Precious Pet of Gold

Mary Ellen Bauer

Copyright © 2024 by Mary Ellen Bauer. 857406

All rights reserved. No part of this book may be reproduced or transmitted in any form or by any means, electronic or mechanical, including photocopying, recording, or by any information storage and retrieval system, without permission in writing from the copyright owner.

This is a work of fiction. Names, characters, places and incidents either are the product of the author's imagination or are used fictitiously, and any resemblance to any actual persons, living or dead, events, or locales is entirely coincidental.

To order additional copies of this book, contact:
Xlibris
844-714-8691
www.Xlibris.com
Orders@Xlibris.com

ISBN:	Softcover	979-8-3694-1302-9
	EBook	979-8-3694-1301-2

Library of Congress Control Number: 2023924266

Print information available on the last page

Rev. date: 01/05/2024

Table of Contents

Chapter 1   Historical Review 1

Chapter 2   Physical Attributes 10

Chapter 3   Medical Highlights 18

Chapter 4   Breeding Procedures 28

Chapter 5   Growth Stages 43

Chapter 6   Character Description 54

Chapter 7   Grooming Techniques 65

Chapter 8   Training Methods 74

Chapter 9   Career Arenas 97

Chapter 10   Rescue Shelters 133

Dedication

The dedication of this book is truly heartfelt for me. My mind and heart pondered our book's dedication for many weeks. Being that my husband and I researched this book as a couple, I was concerned that it may appear inappropriate to dedicate it to my husband. My worries were outweighed by my incredible passion for this remarkable breed and true respect for my loving husband.

Bruce has been a devoted lover of goldens for thirty-two years. His first love, Maxi, taught him just how valuable a golden is in his life. The bond they share shall be one of forever lasting love and respect. She has passed to heaven, but her precious spirit lives within my husband every day of his life.

Personal Reflections

"Max and Me"

His life has revolved around two principles: friendship and hunting. His personal story is based on the old saying, "a dog is a man's best friend". His best friends were his two dogs: Peaches, an English Springer Spaniel mix and Maxie, his golden retriever. The three of them made quite the trio.

It has been an honor to live, learn, and laugh with those ladies. They taught one another a great deal. Their learning experience involved three best friends enjoying more than a few wonderful hunting trips. Hunting requires great skill and tremendous luck; thanks to his dogs, he was honored with both.

Peaches and Bruce were united first. Who'd have guessed that tiny droopy eared pup would grow up to be a champion hunter. She and Bruce learned the hunting ropes paw to hand, hand to paw. English Springers hunt using specific skills and physical features: speed, brush coverage, and smell. They learned a lot about flushing out birds and rabbits. Anyone hungry for some rabbit stew? Have you ever tried Pheasant under glass? Man, his stomach's growling, MMM . . . delicious!

Life marched on; he knew it was time to introduce a new friend. Peaches was still my champ, but she was getting older. It was prime time to put her next best skill to the test. He had no doubt in his mind and heart that his old girl would make an excellent teacher.

I liked Peaches' traits and capabilities but was curious about the differences a golden portrayed. The physical imagery would present a new style or form of hunting. Research indicated that golden retrievers were great for taller grass, the terrain he'd been avoiding due to Peach's shorter legs. Goldens were ranked on the top of the sporting dog list, a well-deserved mark of honor. Hunt clubs and sporting stores raved about the sleek skills of goldens. His mind was made up; it was time to go shopping for his golden pup.

Maxie caught his eye. She looked sharp. Her eyes sparkled with energy and loyalty. She was mine, or in all honesty, ours, She was his, or in all honesty, theirs, he promised Peaches, they'd share her.

His two girls got along great. Peaches enjoyed showing Maxie the ropes. They spent a lot of time in the woods. The combined skill of three master hunters challenged the pheasant population. They were quick to claim their fair share of birds.

The girls would keep their noses peaked. Peach would challenge the lower brush, while Maxie ruled the taller grass. His job was to control his dogs, be gun ready, know his environment, and spot his bird. The girls would search out a bird, flush it out into the open air, and expose it for him to prove his shooting ability. Search, flush, expose, and BOOM; yes, they got their bird.

The girls would watch every move the bird made. They were captivated as it fluttered and dropped from the sky. The race was on, which one would reach the bird first? Peach was very possessive over her birds. She was proud of her hard work. Max was his gentle giant. She'd softly grasp the bird in her mouth and bring it right to his feet. These girls had it going on; he was just the man to mark their hard work a great success.

Nothing revved him up more than when the girls double teamed a bird. Pheasants were not as dumb as some hunters believed. Yes, they got a hot one! The girls would double team to flush the panicked bird. The bird would shift from low tight brush into the tree line. Hoping it had lost the dogs, it would make a sweep for the tall grass to hide. There was no hiding from his dogs. Peach nailed the brush, pushing it into the trees. The bird's nerves panicked it into flight. The tall grass made an excellent cover, not. Max bolted through the grass like a bull in a China shop. The frightened bird took flight in hopes of freedom. His master hunting skills kicked into gear, ready, aim, shoot. Yes, they got their bird. Two kills for the day, perfect success.

Reminiscing brings so many memories to mind. He could share these stories over another hundred pages.

His advice to fellow hunters, follow your heart, know your mind; make the decision right for you. He personally believes a hunter could never go wrong buying, training and hunting a golden, but everyone must feel that drive inside of themselves.

Personal Reflections

"The Old and the New"

Our family is our world. Reflecting upon treasured memories is very important to us. Please join us for a journey through time.

Breanna is our oldest birth child. She was highly spirited from the very point of conception. Our pregnancy was quite nerve-wracking; medical specialists questioned her every moment of development. The day of her birth was more than a miracle; it was the beginning of our parental adventure. Bruce concentrated on Breanna's gorgeous blue eyes. We knew our life would be incredible, seeing the world through the eyes of a child, what a remarkable gift.

Maxie was my husband's first golden retriever. She was beautiful, an English cream with brilliant eyes; her eyes sparkled with joy and love. Many spiritualists believe a dog portrays special eyes; eyes known as the windows to the world. If this could be true; Maxie truly portrayed such eyes. Her heart was filled with loving affection. We were concerned she may have trouble adjusting from being a single man's hunting dog into a family's center of attention, but she ruled it all. She had no problem filling all the shoes asked of her.

Bringing Breanna home from the hospital was exhilarating, but nerve-wracking as well. We were concerned that Maxie would have a problem accepting a new addition to the family. Our concerns were for nothing. Uniting Breanna and Maxie was a blast!

The situation was just the opposite of what we had feared; Maxie adored the new baby. She loved her so much; she adopted her as her very own baby. Breanna, human baby verses golden retriever puppy. Life was a laugh a minute.

We decorated Breanna's nursery, prepared her essentials and organized our schedules. Everything was in perfect order, yeah right! Our daughter never slept; we were exhausted. Bruce would cuddle with her; she slept with daddy and mom because she disliked her basinet. I would sing to her to calm her nerves. Maxie would fetch her necessities to quiet her cries. This baby had the three of us wrapped around her tiny little fingers.

Maxie and Breanna grew together. They were both our babies; remember those girls' eyes! Breanna was mischievous; we had to watch her every move. We knew we could count on Maxie to be a great babysitter. She worked cheap, a few treats, and was totally trustworthy. Honestly, the two made a great pair, Breanna, a.k.a. the devil and Maxie, a.k.a. the angel.

Bruce and I wanted to show Maxie how much we appreciated her help and love. We felt bad about booting her out of our bed; Breanna insisted on sleeping with us, so we just didn't have space for four. It was time to rectify the problem. We decided to buy Maxie a doggy bed of her very own.

Dogs are color blind; of course, humans do not think of that fact. We argued over which color Maxie would like the best. Breanna chose blue, her own favorite color. The flowered one was pretty, but Breanna liked the one with butterflies much more. Three stores and seven doggy beds later, we bought Maxie her new bed.

Maxie was thrilled, oh yeah! She took one look at it and walked away. We moved it room to room, but there was no interesting her in the bed. Bruce thought she may have taken it as the last straw, no fair, the baby comes first. What could we do to make Maxie happy?

We were getting tired. It had been a long day. Bruce had to work the next morning and being busy with my sassy little girl, I was exhausted. Bedtime, Bruce convinced Maxie to rest in her new bed. Breanna cuddled between us. Tick tock, the night slipped away.

The beautiful bright sunshine greeted us with a big surprise. Oh, my heavens, where was Breanna? She had been asleep at midnight when I had checked on her. We rushed around the house searching for her. It was 5:00a.m.; where could she be? Bruce called out in a laugh, "honey, you got to see this". Breanna was cuddled up in Maxie's doggy bed. She looked adorable. Next thought, where was Maxie? She was snuggled up in Breanna's crib. The two shared the nursery quite well, perfect roommates.

The doggy bed was a better investment than we had realized. Bruce and I got our bed to ourselves. Could baby two soon be on the way?

Personal Reflections

"Legacy Lives on"

Tick tock tick tock, the time had come to remember just who was number one. Remembering and honoring Maxi was a critical priority. Bruce's heart required a break from English Cream Goldens; yet maintaining his deep love of Golden Retrievers. The wonderful saying "Time heals all wounds" truly hit home with my husband's broken heart. He could once again enjoy his precious memories of Maxi with a big smile and a vigorous yearning.

An amazing opportunity came knocking at our door. We are proud to say our outstanding reputation amongst the Golden Retriever world was the key to unlock yesterday's pain and turn it into today's blessing. My husband was elated to open his heart and home to yet another incredible English Cream Golden Retriever.

There was no replacing, Maxi; our goal was to honor her outstanding attributes with the addition of an English Cream of outstanding quality and charisma. Introducing Aristotle Matthias Bauer born July 29, 2021. This gorgeous stud was brilliant as well as brave. Aristotle was born from outstanding bloodlines carrying top of the line genetics. His amazing temperament shines through and through expressing his big heart and love for life. We know Maxi would have chosen this gorgeous stud to be her very own.

Our gorgeous young stud put us through our paces. He excelled in all levels of obedience. His intelligence, stamina, and instinctive attributes urged us to place him in the Diabetic service arena. One cannot live for love alone, by this we mean sure he enjoys being a stud, but he needed another job as well. Aristotle's calling was dutifully recognized and highly rewarded as he surpassed great expectations and goals as a diabetic servicer. Our incredible young man deserved the perfect prize for, stud service, and diabetic service both jobs well done.

What do you ask is the perfect prize? We believed it to be a precious princess. The search was on, scheduling meetings with numerous English Cream breeders. We had conducted approximately seventeen interviews before selecting our beautiful Alaura Lee Bauer born April 25, 2022. This gorgeous little girl is quite the lady. Her personality is the perfect mix of sweet and sassy with a lot of spunk and sincerity thrown in for good measure. Alaura loves her stud, and he really worships his little lady. They make the perfect English Cream couple with a great future of puppy making to come.

Maxi shall always represent our great beginning with English Cream Golden Retrievers. She prompted an outstanding timeline of love, loyalty and legacy throughout her life. The great foundation that she has joyfully gifted us shines like the North star guiding us through life. Maxi lovingly shares her mark of gold, forever, for always.

My husband needed time to grieve before we prepared to purchase and raise our current goldens. We researched medical updates, breeding programs, and implemented family bonding as we carefully developed our plan to welcome a new family member into our hearts and home. The selection process was difficult. We were cautious to confirm all data, references, and finances. Our most important issue was to not see or hold a pup until we were sure of the breeding security. The time finally came to purchase our new pup. The drive was exhilarating; our family couldn't wait another minute. My husband fell in love with a gorgeous chubby little girl. I just adored the tiny runt. The kids loved all of the pups. How could we choose just one; well, we couldn't, we welcomed two beautiful females: Abby and Anna into our family.

Selecting our sire was much easier. Our daughter, Breanna urged us to purchase Sir Alexander Kaden Bauer the Great from a close friend of hers. We cross referenced the breeder and confirmed medical and breed records. Alex was quickly adopted into the Bauer family. He knows he is the king.

My husband's love of this breed has drawn two families, the Goldens and the Bauers, together as one. His love, knowledge and skill have granted us a precious gift, the miracle of a golden family.

Personal Reflections

"Dear Abby"

Family life gets very hectic; kids, goldens, work, school, activities, and sleep consume our every minute. Organization plays a key role in our life management. We dedicate our love and attention to each of our family members; admittedly; however, sometimes, we simply run out of time and energy. Oops; someone accidently got forgotten!

Golden retrievers are very similar to children; their minds need to be active and their hearts demand coddling. Abagale craved attention and exercise, which she usually got plenty of; however, there was no competing with her spring fever.

A quick game of fetch just didn't cut it. She adored her belly rub, but 10 minutes was only a start. Tossing a treat or two was nothing more than a big tease. Abby gave up on human satisfaction; she was on the "hunt" for her own fun, in other words, she was looking for trouble.

Preoccupied wasn't the word for our day. Our jobs devoured our day. Kids stole our last bit of energy. We were so exhausted that we were just about to order pizza because we were too tired to make dinner. Everyone voted for fast food, even Abby.

Well, Abby had her own theory on "fast food", how about rabbit stew? No Way! Abby didn't want to carry out, delivery, or to go out for dinner; she brought it right to our feet. Talk about "fast"!

Our goofy hunting dog went hunting without her hunter. Quite honestly, Bruce was a bit jealous that she had found time for hunting and he didn't get to go along. Abby had after dinner plans; she wanted to run her own newspaper ad, "wanted master hunter to accompany great hunting dog on super fun hunting trips; my owner is too busy to go".

Are you familiar with the term "soft mouthed"? This term refers to a golden grasping things with their mouth in a soft manner, as to not damage or tear it. Our golden girl was definitely, "soft mouthed", an excellent hunting trait. She sure proved her skill; I attempted to pick the bunny up from our porch and got the surprise of my life; it hopped away! Thank goodness it was still alive; I on the other hand almost died of a heart attack. Wow, Abby's idea of fast food is too fast for me!

Chapter 1

Historical Review

Golden retrievers enjoy a truly honorable history. Allow them to travel through time. Please pack your intellectual suitcase and prepare for an incredible journey.

Scotland has been recognized as the home of origin for the golden retriever. They have been successfully dated as far back as the mid-18th century. Records indicate bloodlines may be traced to the breed entitled, water spaniels. Breeders conducted numerous cross breeding's of predated early retrievers and water spaniels in search of producing the perfect dog.

Master breeders were searching to provide owners with the following breed traits: superior retrieving skills, terrain management capabilities, and significant hunting skills. Top breeders gleamed with success; pleasuring skilled hunters with a "side kick", a master hunting tool, the new breed of master hunting dog fully capable of working the water struck terrain, as well as conquering the hardships presented on land. A unique blending of skills and talents quickly earned these breeders the "mark of gold", an honor which would travel through time.

Stories expressing great prestige graced the growing communities. Guests from Great Britain were overwhelmed with curiosity; earnestly craving more knowledge and personal contact with this wonderful dog. Sharing intellectual respect and personal appreciation led to a massive news flash "the goldens were coming".

This immaculate breed was proudly welcomed by the British. The kennel club of England opened registration for golden retrievers as flat coat-goldens in 1903. Outstanding advancements flooded the dog arena; 1908 honored the exhibiting of the flat coat–golden, later leading to the recognition as being a breed described as retrievers (golden and yellow), an honor announced in 1911. British breeders were quite proud. Selective breeding programs encouraged the successful promotion of this breed, not only within the British arena, but once again forged it on to yet another land.

Golden retrievers are hosting a country-to-country tour; shall we enjoy an American view? Impeccable traits noted as: loyal, skilled and adaptable were quick to prove its worthiness. Goldens were inducted into the American Kennel Club in 1925. This great accomplishment led to yet another great mark in time, the founding of the Golden Retriever Club of America in 1938. This gorgeous breed beholding remarkable capabilities had truly won the heart of America;

their gracious presence shall carry profound reflections from the breed's prominently noted yesteryears as it successfully continues to dominate the world of sporting dogs in the future.

Prominent Americans raved over the glory of this precious dog breed. Top line kennels continued selective breeding programs to assure the superior quality of the goldens. Master breeders once again enjoyed a significant "pat on the back" from yet another admirer, Canada.

Canada warmly welcomed this glowing breed in 1927, the year noting the breed's induction into the Canadian Kennel Club. This glorious honor assisted in the development of the Golden Retriever Club of Ontario, recently restated as the Golden Retriever Club of Canada, formed in 1958. This loving country, along with a long list of preceding lands proudly cheers this precious breed, the golden retriever.

Personal Reflections

"Why Me?"

Selecting a golden retriever may be either a very personal or strictly a professional decision. Regardless of the purpose of the choice, this decision involves a great deal of processing and consideration. Research, contemplate, prepare, and confirm all issues of puppy purchasing before jumping into buying any pup or dog.

Golden retrievers exhibit prominent traits: strength, loyalty, speed, intelligence, and endurance. They place high in the sporting dog world, proving tremendous capability as excellent: trackers, hunters, companions, and service workers. The skills produced by years of master breeding are proudly honored throughout time; thus, welcoming the breed into the many arenas of today.

Once the breed selection itself has been confirmed, one must determine which arena or field of placement the golden is requested to serve. One individual may choose to employ a golden as a watchdog, whereas another person may be searching for the perfect family dog. Role placement is vital to the health and life of the dog as it matures and trains. Goldens are very intellectual and energetic dogs; preparing a life plan which promotes the talents and skills of the dog being used in their most constructive and productive manner leads to the development of a successful life.

My husband's first true love was not me, no way, she was his golden retriever, Maxie. Bruce had spent a great deal of time researching goldens before selecting the breed. The second point in breed selecting was to pinpoint the role she would portray in his life. This role was obvious, hunting. He, being an avid hunter, knew exactly which traits and skills he was searching for in a dog.

Maxie's blood lines proved strong hunting capabilities. The lineage report was remarkable; genetics indicated she had what it took, now structure those instincts and talents into master skills. Bruce and Maxie enjoyed several hours of training along the road to hunting success.

Historically, hunters demanded dogs capable of great terrain endurance, a skill or trait yearned for by hunters of today. Maxie honored her heritage by proving her strengths in the field. She had what it took and she knew how to use it. Tracking, flushing, and retrieving skills implemented by master hunting dogs. This young lady earned the gold in golden retriever.

Breeding Maxie was our responsibility, not simply our choice. We were very aware of just how powerful her breed markers truly were in the golden retriever market. Future golden owners deserved the pleasure and privilege of her bloodlines. We were proud to continue producing pups of such tremendous quality.

Maxie's life had been dedicated to hunting, but we knew the same traits that developed a master hunter could be implemented in many additional arenas. The selective breeding process that created our precious Maxie would be put to work once again. We cautiously chose a sire; this young man had to be a product of superior quality. The marriage of Maxie and Tank would assure the birth of yet another superior line. These pups would honor society with their talents, skills, and capabilities. What an incredible gift.

The pups truly were a miracle; in all honesty, they would become more of a treasure than we could have ever forecasted. Our very first-born female, Lady, began her relocation with a young family who trained her as a search and rescue worker with the California Coast Guard, an arena perfecting traits once known to hunting dogs alone.

Maxie birthed a large cream male, later named Zeus. This pup was gorgeous, calm, and intelligent. We considered keeping him, but an interested party convinced us that his son needed, not only wanted this pup. The young boy had a disease entitled multiple sclerosis. The family provided two years of service training to develop this pup into a highly skilled service dog for the boy's medical and personal aid.

A third pup born of this litter was a medium golden female, somewhat smaller, very energetic, and quite intelligent. Introducing Miss Daisy. This young lady touched the therapy arena as a long term welcomed visitor at the new owner's wife's nursing care facility. The pup received great obedience training, allowing her to develop wonderful therapy skills. Visiting his wife at such a place was uncomfortable for the sad husband. The pup provided stress relief, a loving companion who not only attended the visit, but went home to comfort the lonely friend. Litter to litter, Maxie's love of life traveled through time.

We have patterned all our pup purchases after the success of Maxie. It is truly worth the work put into selection. There is so much more to a puppy than its cuteness or instant adorability. Pups grow up into a dog. Owners must look back upon the breed history to see the dog's future possibilities. Loving goldens has truly been an honorable walk along a golden pathway through time.

Chapter 2
Physical Attributes

Physical attributes may include the following discussion: breed types, physical confirmation, color specifications, and breed temperament. Please note: each category requires a breakdown of specific factors within the presented subject. The following paragraphs shall highlight materials directly linked to the introductory arenas.

Golden retriever breed types may be listed as the following: British, American, and Canadian. These breed types have been founded based on specifications demanded by the country of origin. British goldens may highlight such traits as: wide short muzzle, block style forehead, deeper chest, shorter legs, and shorter tail. British goldens are a bit larger in size; males measuring 56–61 cm. at the withers, whereas females measure 51-56 cm. at withers. Weight standards have not been addressed; therefore, cannot be discussed. British Kennel Club standards state a requirement of a level top line and straight hind quarters without allotting for the angulation noted in American lines. European type may note darker and rounder eyes. Color standards for this type may reflect golden highlights and cream variations. Red and mahogany are not allowed under the breed club standards. Cream variations were once a negative feature; however, thanks to the public's positive demands, it is now a welcomed feature. British goldens are honored for their muscular physique and outstanding confirmation.

American golden retrievers may be promoted for qualities designated to their specific type: triangular shaped eyes, water repellent dense coat, moderate feathering, smooth gait, balanced limbs, and rounded shoulders. Measurements of this type may be stated as: males: 56–61 cm. at the withers, whereas females may measure 51-56 cm. at the withers. American type coats may indicate various shades of brilliant goldens. American Kennel Club standards do not permit white, black, or red in confirmation judging. Judges may disqualify goldens portraying pink noses or lack of pigment. Judges are trusted for their professional discretion in the confirmation arena. American type goldens are highly revered for their unique attractiveness and capabilities.

Canadian type may host the following breed traits: deep set eyes, rounded shoulders, balanced hips, shallow facials, narrowed muzzle, thin coat, long tail, lanky status, thin necks, and strong legs. Measurements may be stated as: males may average 58–62 cm. at his withers, whereas a female may measure 52–57 cm. at her withers. Coat variations indicate a thinner and darker coat. Canadian golden retrievers are skillful hunters, qualified show participants, and remarkable pets; thus, placing the breed third amongst the sporting dog industry throughout Canada.

Breed types share many similarities: gentle temperament, impeccable intelligence and attractive appearance. The variations presented may highlight noteworthy specifications; however, promote the solidity of the breed overall. Goldens of all types are strong, loyal, intelligent dogs with tremendous capabilities. Society as a whole is honored to welcome the grand reputation revered by this master breed.

Personal Reflection

"Handing down the crown"

Bong, bong boldly strikes the prestigious grandfather clock, as we cheerfully yet reluctantly celebrate our sire's eleventh birthday; the day had come to bow our heads in respect and with gratitude to our amazing stud Sir Alexander Kaden Bauer the great. He truly is a living legend. Though he shall always be our King, the time had come to search for our Prince.

The search was on! Step one was to determine a list of characteristics we required of our perfect Prince: deep red coat, genetically sound bloodline, loving playful temperament, and of course respectful financial foundation. We began interviewing breeders across the Midwest; this process was an absolute must because it provided us with invaluable breeder portfolios, bloodline facts, and bonding opportunities. Admittedly, many breeders denied interviews because they felt our requests and requirements were much too stringent. Bauer family goldens was in search of perfection; however, we never dreamt this search would become a yearlong journey. Luckily, our adventure earned us the greatest treasure, the purchase of our amazing Prince.

Introducing Abu Logan Bauer, a truly amazing golden retriever pup beholding exemplary traits bar none. This selection process was one unique adventure our family will never forget. Four very nice golden retriever stud pups and their breeders endured our intense interviewing requirements. Choosing one of these four great pups would prove to be a grueling chore. Fine tuning our list of requirements would mean a strict breakdown of each and every characteristic we were searching for in a pup. The first and foremost requirement was to assure the bloodlines were of the highest quality. Abu's heritage is wonderful. The second demand was that Abu must carry excellent temperament; three visits to play with this pup and his parents assured us that he had the most playful and kindest attitude of all four pups. Let us not be vain yet it must be noted that good looks mean a great deal when choosing a sire pup; all we can say is "Looking good, looking good" wow this young stud had it going on and keeps it going! The financial package involved in Abu's purchase was very respectful; though this young stud was in Minnesota and our visitation required a great deal of winter travel he has proven to be worth every dime.

Our scenario definitely didn't follow "out with the old" Sir Alexander Kaden Bauer the great and "in with the new" Abu Logan Bauer, it actually took the direction of "learn from the best". Alexander fulfilling the roles of golden professor took his teaching job very seriously as he enjoyed teaching the new pup a few tricks and skills. Everyone enjoyed watching Alexander and his new shadow as they ran around the yard welcoming new adventures.

Chapter 3

Medical Highlights

Medical highlights are a vital part of a golden retriever's health regiment. Significant attention must be dedicated to these designated issues: hip dysplasia, elbow dysplasia, cancer forms, cataracts, muscular dystrophy, hypothyroidism, insulinoma, myasthenia gravis, mucocutaneous, hypopigmentation, pericardial effusion, progressive retinal atrophy, obesity, skin disorders and subaortic stenosis. Please note the following paragraphs for a brief discussion; more details may be highlighted by referencing additional professional resources.

Hip dysplasia is a common disorder described as abnormal development or degeneration of one or both hip joints. The hips are actually ball and socket joints in which the head of each specific femur unites with the concave socket of the pelvic bone. The abnormal development of tissues, bones, organs and/or other structures create points of disturbance. Genetics play a valid role in this medical arena. Dislocation may result if the head of the femur is too loose causing: abnormal mechanical forces across the hip, irregularly shaped bones, damaged cartilage, microscopic bone fractures, and at outside cases, degenerative joint disease. Young dogs may also face this hardship; it is most likely to occur when confirmational abnormalities cause a poor fit between the head of the femur and the pelvic acetabulum which therefore results in hip laxity. Older dogs suffer this tragedy when progressive hip degeneration and deterioration of bone and cartilage within the hip joint become serious. Genetics influence all cases of this issue. Additional causes may be noted as: nutritional and environmental factors. For example, obesity and trauma play significant roles in this medical tragedy.

Medical specialists conduct x-rays to view the conditions of the hips throughout the stages of a dog's life. Prevention of this critical disorder may begin with medical screenings. Dogs noted with this problem must be removed from breeding programs or withdrawn from breeding status. Dietary care provides a strong sense of caution; nutritionally appropriate food and treats should be selected. Weight management is a wonderful precaution for hip dysplasia. Moderate exercise and limited stunts is a must in the prevention of hip dysplasia. Pups should limit jumping, standing on rear legs, and excessive leaping as these activities may cause hip problems. Mild discomfort on one or both rear legs becomes noticeable when hip issues begin. This discomfort will graduate to pain and hardship with walking or maneuvering. Limping, shifting, tiring, and stumbling are signs of hip troubles. Owners may highlight the following list of signs; hind limb lameness, abnormal "bunny hopping" gate, hind leg weakness, hip or pelvic pain, reluctance to stand or reposition, extreme stiffness, activity reduction, painful grinding, loud clicking, narrowed high end stance, poor rear conformation, shrinking of high-end muscles, enlargement of shoulder muscles, and arched back from extended hocks. The incredible hardships endured by dogs struck with hip dysplasia are saddening.

Therapeutically goals involve: pain relief, stabilize hip joints, improve mechanical joint function, decrease progression, and ultimately return the dog to normal capabilities.

Treatment and management programs may call for numerous surgical procedures; this is not an answer in all cases and may result in further issues. Mild cases of hip dysplasia may call for non-surgical treatments: physical therapy, hydrotherapy, dietary management, weight control, exercise restriction, and use of medications. Nontraditional therapy programs may be listed as: massage therapy, acupuncture techniques, acupressure techniques, surgical implantation of gold beads, herbal remedies, and additional wellness promotion methods. Veterinarians must be contacted for a complete medical review.

Elbow dysplasia is a terrible problem for golden retrievers. This dysfunction or disease may be described by explaining what the elbow is and what it is capable of performing. The elbow is a joint. It connects the long bone to the upper front leg to the two long bones of the lower front leg. The elbow is capable of tremendous versatility. It beholds a hinging capability as well as a rotating ability. Elbow dysplasia takes place when the abnormal development of size, shape, and organization of cells, tissues, organs, bones, or additional body structures affects the performance of the elbow.

Elbow dysplasia may lead to numerous health conditions: foreleg lameness, arthritis, and joint deterioration. This problem is primarily a genetic issue. It may be associated with rapid growth patterns and high protein diets. Signs of this dysfunction may include discomfort, pain, limping, stiffness, and exhaustion. The diagnosis must be conducted by a veterinarian.

Treatment options may vary. Surgical versus non-surgical options are discussed once an appropriate diagnosis has been determined. Arthroscopy techniques are one of the leading procedures used for the treatment of elbow dysplasia. Non-surgical methods may include: medications, physical therapy, massage therapy, cold packing, exercise reduction, and life plan monitoring. All care selections or procedures must be guided by a medical specialist.

Cancer is a heart wrenching subject facing humans and dogs alike. "Cancer is defined as any malignant cellular tumor" defines www.PetWave.com. A tumor is a swollen region or collection of tissues holding uncontrolled cell and progressive mutation. Tumors may be classified in one of two categories: benign or malignant. Benign tumors are not cancerous. Malignant tumors are cancerous. Cancer may be described as a progressive development of abnormal tissues which transfer throughout the body.

Golden retrievers are susceptible to many types of cancer. These cancers may be listed as: lymph sarcoma, osteosarcoma, soft tissue sarcomas, mast cell tumors, hemangiosarcoma, oral melanoma, and mammary neoplastic. These cancers may inflict a golden retriever in unique extremes. The cause of cancer has not yet been identified.

Medical experts must conduct specialized tests before diagnosing cancer issues. Once a dog has been tested appropriate treatments may be designated. Dogs that are tested cancer free are very fortunate, but future testing should be considered for the dog's protection. Dogs facing a positive cancer diagnosis may consider numerous treatment plans. The first step in cancer treatment is to seek quality medical prevention care. Veterinarian visits should be prompt. It is important to seek the care of superior medical experts when attempting to diagnose your golden. Treatments are usually based on the determination of cancer type specification. Once a medical expert has defined the type of cancer, specifications regarding treatment may follow. Treatments may include, but not be limited to, the following: surgery, radiation, chemotherapy, medication, targeted molecular therapy, immunotherapy, hyperthermia, cry-therapy, phototherapy, photo-chemotherapy, thermo-chemotherapy and emerging unconventional or alternative therapies. New wave treatments may include massage therapies, acupuncture, and acupressure techniques. Herbal supplements have also gained attention in recent years. Regardless of which treatment is chosen, all owners, handlers, breeders, and veterinarians seek to save the life of their beloved dog. Providing medical care with love and success is the unified goal of all dog lovers.

Cataracts are defined as any opacity of the lens of the dog's eye. This problem is not gender specific. Senior goldens are more likely to face this issue. This medical hardship will create a lack of vision. Severe cases may lead to blindness. There are selective causes of this medical problem: genetics, nutrition deficiencies, low blood calcium levels, toxin exposure, diabetes (mellitus), radiation, electric shock, and blunt or penetrating trauma. This disease may appear with no onset reasoning. The formal biological cause is labeled as the change of the protein composition and or arrangement of the eye's lens fibers. Prevention is limited; removal of affected dogs is helpful, but not a sure remedy. Visual screening is useful, but once again it is not a guarantee of safety. Testing may involve a reassessment of dogs' pupillary light reflexes, menace reflexes, visual reactions, blood screening, and glucose testing as well as several in depth screenings. Please research superior medical resources for detailed information regarding testing procedures.

Surgical treatment is highly successful for goldens who are diagnoses during the early onset of this disease. Dogs who cannot be treated adjust well to the visual issues they must face. Specialist's state at additional physical hardship is not common because of cataracts. Goldens should be handled with tender loving care throughout the discomfort of this health issue.

Muscular dystrophy is a serious health issue in many dog breeds. Goldens have coped with this problem for years but have been fortunate in that recent research has produced significant advancements in the awareness of this health hardship. Please note medical digests or medical experts for details regarding this issue.

Hypothyroidism, a serious syndrome caused by inadequate production and release of the thyroid hormones triiodothyronie(t3) and thyroxin(t4), which are required for normal metabolic functions in the body. Symptoms of this disease are various and are nonspecific. Hypothyroidism is easily diagnosed. This common disease is usually caused by lymphocytic thyroiditis or idiopathic thyroid glands atrophy. These harsh conditions must involve immune – medicated destruction of or damage to the thyroid glands. Experts have determined that the dogs' immunologic defense mechanisms target the dogs' own thyroid tissues; therefore, assaulting their own system as though it was an enemy. Circulating t3 and t4 levels diminish, resulting in a cascade of metabolic abnormalities. Secondary Hypothyroidism is very rare in dogs. This is usually a result of congenital disease, pituitary gland disease, dietary iodine deficiency, space-occupying pituitary tumors, or additional abnormalities.

Prevention is quite rare if not impossible. Diagnosis is very easy as recent research and testing procedures are very successful. Treatments involve the application of oral medications. Dogs must cope with treatment throughout the balance of their life span. Maintaining appropriate thyroid levels will support a healthy regiment for the dog. Providing superior care will grant the dog a much healthier and happier life.

Progressive retinal atrophy refers to a group of degenerative eye disorders which may lead to permanent blindness. The retina is a thin membrane lining the back of the dogs' eyes. The retina absorbs and reflects light. Damaged retinas cannot complete their appointed function.

The cause of this disease is questionable. Genetics have been targeted. Prevention includes prescreening and genetic monitoring of genetic history. Diagnoses are placed on the shoulders of specialists. Experts use an electroretinogram to measure the retinas capability to respond to light. Sadly, this disease is not treatable.

Obesity is stated as an abundance of 20% above the appropriate body weight. Maintaining correct weight levels for goldens is very important. Veterinarians will conduct a weight measurement and touch the dog for hands on examination. A dog's ribs should be well felt, but not overly expressive. Dogs should not exhibit fat rolls. Obese dogs may suffer breathing hardships. Dogs carrying excessive weight are less playful or active. Prevention of this issue is a serious matter. Dogs should perform an appropriate exercise schedule. Dietary regiments are vital as a means of prevention as well as for treatment of disease. The term "moderation" is the key to preventing and treating this massive disease. Seek professional care for appropriate medical programs.

Skin disorders are numerous in range. The listing of all skin disorders is massive. Please seek advanced medical materials for a complete report regarding this field. Prevention, diagnosis, causes and treatments are based on the specific skin disorder. Dogs cope with a wide variety of these issues. Health maintenance regarding this matter is a must.

The following health issues: insulinoma, myasthenia gravis, hock osteochondrosis, mucocutaneous, hypopigmentation, pericardial effusion, and subaorticstenosis are all serious issues which may harm a golden retriever. Medical information may be researched by contacting superior references and professionals within the specific fields of medicine.

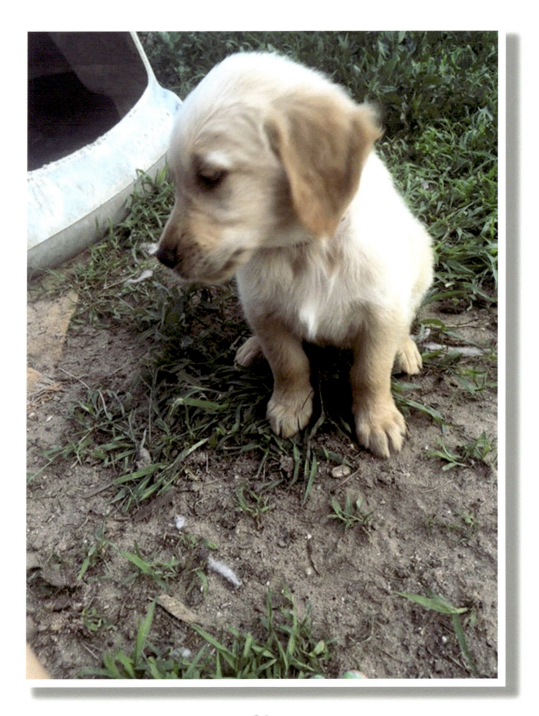

Personal Reflection

"My Diet Buddy"

I hate diets. Counting calories is such a chore. Comparing diet programs is a headache in the making. I just couldn't do it alone; I needed a diet buddy!

The first step was to connect with my friends. How do I ask a friend if she/he would like to diet with me, without offending someone? I wanted to be considerate to everyone, but searching for the right person was like walking on eggshells; I guess that's better than walking on someone's feelings. Two weeks passed and no takers. What's a very overweight desperate woman to do? Who is man's best friend? Who is this woman's best friend? Who better to buddy up with, my gorgeous, golden, Anastacia?

Anastacia and I took dieting very seriously. We had a deal; she and I agreed to share everything. I thought that if she ate half of my food, I'd only consume half of the calories; therefore, lose weight. Great idea, right! Who needs to portion food, half and half seemed reasonable. Count actual calories, why bother, I couldn't be eating that much, after all, Anna ate half. Buy diet foods, no way, Anna won't eat that stuff; what kind of buddy would I be if I bought food both of us didn't like. Anna was more than willing to share her dog food, yuck, eew, no way! Seriously, I did not give her people food; dogs require healthy nutrition for a healthy life. Above all, I love her too much to ask her to eat diet food. This diet program grew more lax every day.

I spent a week planning this out. She made the perfect buddy. First of all; she wouldn't, ha ha, couldn't tell on me for cheating on my diet. She would eat the diet food I disliked, yeah right! Best of all; she couldn't read the scale. What did it say; I lost 19 lbs, "dreaming"!

I was in heaven; that was until I had to get weighed in at my doctor's office; I had forgotten that part. Reality check, one can cheat on a diet, but no one can cheat the scale. Boohoo, naughty me, busted!

Anna definitely got the better deal. Cheating on a diet means the dieter cheats on themselves, double the ouch. I got my butt kicked. Who would be taking who for a walk in the park from now on!

Chapter 4

Breeding Procedures

Dogs are creatures of nature. Female goldens endure puberty similar to human youths and teenagers. The dog will experience heat cycles, a time during which their bodies physically produce eggs for reproduction. Heat cycles usually last about three weeks. There are three stages: preparing, servicing, and pregnancy.

Owners will notice swelling of the dog's volva and a bloody discharge during the first stage of preparation. She is not releasing eggs during this part of her heat. Male dogs will be chemically drawn to the female; however, she will show no or little interest in the male. This stage lasts about six to eleven days.

Fertility will begin during the second stage of heat. The bloody discharge will alter color, light pink to a bright golden, indicating her egg dismissal. The volva will soften, inviting a guest, the male. This stage usually lasts five to nine days. The termination of stage two will also end the appreciation of a male's attention.

Stage three will begin with a serious hormonal sharpness. This stage is actually an indication of pregnancy. Females not becoming pregnant will return to normal behavior. Those becoming pregnant will show the following signs: decreased appetite, (human morning sickness), decreased energy, nipple growth, increased irritability, and behavioral changes. Golden mothers usually crave increased attention; whereas, other breeds report requesting more private or alone time. Hormones cause the female to alter her once normal actions. Pregnancy in dogs lasts 60 to 64 days. The pregnant dog will show an increase in appetite about two weeks into her pregnancy. Her weight will increase, exposing a larger and firmer belly; by the way, it is a belly inviting numerous belly rubs. Puppy movement will be noticed during the last week of pregnancy. Many moms drop a few squirts of milk as they prepare to feed their litter.

This stage of pregnancy is the time period owners or breeders refer to as "the babies are coming, get ready" stage. Breeders or owners should preset a whelping box or nesting zone for the mother's comfort and security. The mother will select her own area if none is preset. Do not be amazed if the expectant mother invades the closet or squeezes under her favorite bed; these places provide her with security and contentment.

Expectant mothers may play tricks on owners and breeders. Monitor mothers very carefully. New moms have been known to deliver in unusual locations. The due date is not an exact science; keep a close eye on the mommy to be.

The onset of labor may be predicted once the mother has been pregnant for 58 to 64 days. Signs of labor will include a variation in her temperature. Goldens temperature is usually 101°F to 102°F. Expectant goldens will decrease to 99°F to 97°F; this is a strong indication of an onset of labor.

Labor has three stages. Each stage is repeated with each pup she delivers. Please seek the advice and aid of a professional if any feelings of insecurity or concern arise.

Stage one will expose the mother's irritability. She is coping with nervousness and concerns. She will not want food or treats. We highly recommend taking her out for one last potty break at this point. Many mothers prefer to be left alone to cope with their bodies.

Stage two of labor will be highlighted with the beginning of contractions. She will dismiss a green sack of fluid, a preset before the dismissal of pup sacks. Pups may be born head or rear first; it does not matter which is shown first. The mother will break the sack to release the pup. She will lick or clean the pup; thus, prompting the pup to react with whining or squirming, signs of healthy life. The mother will sever the umbilical cord. Human aid may be called upon if the mother is suffering issues.

Please note the following list of possible complications: lodged puppies, two hours of laboring without any delivery, four hour spread between pup deliveries, delivery does not start after she has dismissed the greenish fluid, late delivery past 65 days of pregnancy, tremor issues occur, onset of vomiting, and excessive panting. Close attention must be delegated to the mother throughout her entire birthing experience. Be prepared to contact an expert for care.

The breeder or owner may assist if the mother is in need of having a pup removed that is stuck. Grip the sack firmly and gently pull the sack out. Place it down for the mother to break the sack. Pups should be removed from the sack immediately; if too much time has elapsed, remove the pup from its sack and place it by its mom. The breeder and owner may use a clean, soft cloth to massage the pup to prompt reaction. Medical emergencies should be reported to the veterinarian for advice and aid.

Stage three of birthing is the resting period. The mother needs to enjoy her pups for a moment. She should be calm and content. The mild contractions will fade out during this stage. This stage is usually an hour or more. The cycles will rotate with the birth of each pup, ending with the birth of the last puppy. Congratulations, she is a mom; introducing a proud new golden litter.

Litter care is vital. Everyone adores puppies, but let us not forget about our precious mother. Mommy needs care and attention as well. Monitoring her nipples is very important; clean her nipples, check for infections, gage milk flow, and keep pup's nails trimmed to prevent scratching or tearing. Soft stool is to be expected for a few weeks; this is a result of physical changes within her body, cleansing her pups, and an alteration in her diet. Minor vaginal discharge is expected for one week; additional discharge should be reported. Territorial or aggressive behavior is normal for new mothers; follow socialization methods as recommended by a professional in the breeding industry.

We suggest the following methods

1. **Slowly approach the mother during labor**
2. **Crouch or sit near her during her labor**
3. **Remain quiet, but talk to her in a friendly voice.**
4. **Attempt to pet her or scratch her ears.**
5. **Do not touch pups during delivery, unless a risk is noted.**
6. **Limit the number of people allowed near the mother for the first few days.**
7. **The owner or breeder should be present when new or different individuals enter the area.**
8. **The owner or breeder should introduce the second person in a friendly voice.**

9. **The second or third guest should not touch the mother until her owner has made the initial contact.**

10. **Owners and familiar guests may begin touching the mother and pups once a loving and secure relationship is established.**

We must bring up a very serious point; golden females will show severe aggression during heat, pregnancy, and new motherhood. The form of aggression is labeled inter-dog aggression. This issue is due to hormones which are irritated throughout these stages. Bitch on bitch aggression is a critical problem. Females may show signs of aggression as early as stage one of heat. The females will show aggression signs: growling, hair raising, biting, and in many cases full contact fighting. Goldens have been known to fight to their death. Many litters have been lost due to excessive aggression. Great caution must be implemented throughout the stages of breeding. This aggression is not normal aggression and therefore, cannot be dealt with in the same manners as typical aggression.

Breeding golden retrievers entails a strong link between medical knowledge and medical ethics. Dog breeding may fall under two divisions: professional and non-professional. Professional breeders own kennels housing selective breeding programs. Master breeders or professional breeders conduct their kennel as a serious business. Nonprofessional breeders include individuals, couples or families who have chosen to welcome golden retriever breeding into their home. Regardless of which status of breeding, all breeders are urged to implement the following breeding standards:

BREED STANDARDS

1. **Complete a review of the breeding sire and dame to assure each are of appropriate temperament. Goldens are honored by their loving and gentle temperament; however there are exceptions to the rule; therefore, it is urged to confirm the parents' temperament before arranging a breeding schedule. Golden retriever bitches are very temperamental during heat cycles and pregnancy; hormones strongly affect the dog's temperament during this time period; the dame should not be judged with aggressive temperament during this time period, rather testing should be conducted during non-active breeding times.**

2. **It is strongly recommended that the breed dog honors the breed standard requirements of the Golden Retriever Club of America.**

3. The breed dog should be a minimum of two years of age and a maximum of eight years of age. Dogs within this age range have the appropriate health to produce a healthy litter.

4. Hip certification is strongly recommended. The orthopedic Foundation of America requires specialized testing, a series of x-rays, indicating the condition of the dog's hips. Dogs receiving a rank of "excellent", "good", or "fair" are acceptable for breeding success. Dogs receiving marks outside of this range should not be used as breed stock.

5. **Dogs should be examined by a Board Certified Ophthalmologist to assure the breed dog is free of hereditary eye disease and or cataracts. Experts conducting these tests must report all results through the Canine Eye Registration Foundation.**

6. **Breeders are prompted to complete heart testing with a Board Certified Cardiologist to assure the breed dog is free of any and all heart issues. The results of all testings should be recorded with the National Heart Registry, which is currently being established thanks to the prompting of golden retriever enthusiasts. This testing regiment may be conducted once the pup reaches one year of age.**

7. The breed dog should have been subject to a thorough medical examination. This examination should include: x-ray series, lab tables and a hands on physical. A family lineage report should accompany this report.

8. Breeding cycles should be investigated. Veterinarians recommend alternating breeding cycles; however, research as indicated that successive cycle breeding may be healthy for young adults in specific cases. Experts prefer to alternate breeding cycles, thus granting a rest period to the dame. This allows her body to recover from the breeding, pregnancy, and mothering roles.

9. **Breeders may be urged to provide proof of accomplishments: show arena: obedience, conformation, and agility competitions: field and hunt, commercial: career portfolio and public notoriety and family lineage reports of prier successors.**

10. **Breeders must supply healthy housing provisions. Whelping boxes, secure pens and/or a clean healthy bed is required for a pregnant goldens safety as she: carries, births, and mothers her litter.**

Once the dame has been serviced, the breeder must respect all pregnancy, delivery, and litter demands. The pregnant dame shall be treated as royalty. Golden retriever mothers enjoy pampering at all times, but truly yearn for it throughout their maternal phases. Please note and consider the following litter responsibilities:

LITTER RESPONSIBILITIES

1. **Selecting top quality dames and sires is vital to superior litter production.**
2. **Providing expert medical care throughout the pregnancy, birthing, and litter beginning is an absolute must.**
3. **Breeders must be financially secure, as to provide financial support for all litter necessities.**
4. **Breeders must emotionally, financially, and medically prepare for all circumstances which may confront the bitch or litter.**
5. **Breeders must be prepared to lose the mother in seriously complicated cases.**
6. **Breeders may have to cope with hand raising the litter if complications occur.**
7. **Provision of suggested worming's and inoculations is highly prompted.**
8. **The dame and litter must be granted top quality nutrition; appropriate food and treats should be carefully monitored.**
9. **A secure setting should be provided for the bitch and litter.**

10. **Socialization is vital during the litters growth and development.**

11. **Superior health charts for size, weight, and inoculations must be maintained throughout the litter's beginning.**

12. **Respecting litter stage development is a must for promoting healthy growth.**

13. **Pups are like human children; they may be sold; the kids may move away, but the parent respectfully honors their responsibilities throughout the life span of the youth.**

14. **Relocation, rehousing, or sale responsibilities are to be honored with the utmost respect. Pup buyers should be subject to the completion of a strict application, face to face interview, and reference check. Buyers should complete superior research regarding the pup they are purchasing. Responsible buyers make respectful owners. Waiting lists are to be expected, as reputable breeders do not mass produce their litters and provide selectively bred pups of top quality.**

Stud dog owners must respect breeding regulations as well. The safety of the dame being serviced must be honored. Stud owners should provide a secure setting for the servicing of the dame; studs traveling to the dame's site should receive similar considerations. The stud owner should assure the stud to be of gentle temperament; aggressive studs may harm the dame. Studs should pass a pre-required physical detailing the stud's physical and emotional health. Stud owners should be prepared to take responsibility for the litter; circumstances may be presented which require stud owners to step in and assume care for the litter. For example, a breeder who has lost the mother in delivery may emotionally turn to the stud owner for assistance or support towards hand raising the pups. A second example may rear in cases involving a breeder facing placement issues; assistance in relocating pups may be requested. Regardless of the reasoning, stud owners should be ready and willing litter caregivers.

Buyers should be cautious of breeders regardless of status: professional or nonprofessional. Research must be adequately conducted before purchasing a pup. Please note the recommendations listed below:

BUYERS GUIDE

1. **Interested buyers should educate themselves on personal breed preferences. Breed information may be obtained through the American Kennel Club, Golden Retriever Club of America, medical experts, numerous literature and medical conferences; a well-educated buyer is a qualified buyer.**

2. **Buyers should thoroughly investigate the breeder they are purchasing from. Request proof of medical records, family lineage, kennel or housing provisions, and certificates or proof of accomplishments on behalf of the pup's family.**

3. **Buyers should perform a hands-on inspection of litter parents. Studs or dames not on sight should be provided for secondary inspection.**

4. **Buyers may request references of pup owners from previously purchased pups. These references may be written or live contacts willing to provide information regarding their pup's status.**

5. **Breeders should provide breed information assuring the buyers knowledge of the breed.**

6. **Buyers should complete an application highlighting their abilities to secure a healthy loving home for the pup. Specifications may include: housing provisions, medical expert references, financial capabilities, and personal contacts. Family screening, career arenas of placement, previous ownership situations, and a review of dog awareness should be seriously approached to secure a healthy home for the golden pup.**

Personal Reflection

"Birthdays"

"Happy Birthday", to Anna's amazing golden retriever puppies! Our hearts just flittered with joy. They were so precious.

Have you ever been present during a dog's birthing? The entire process is just captivating. Birthing is literally a miracle in the making. We were so blessed to be welcomed guests to the birthing of Anastacia's second litter.

My goldens and I are very close. My life revolves around my family of human children and my family of golden retrievers; I dearly treasure them all. Anastacia, our beautiful golden had begun showing signs of labor: temperature drop, appetite decrease, nervous irritability, and finally a green discharge. Ready or not here come the goldens.

Breanna and I spent a great deal of time comforting our mother to be. We caressed her back, scratched her ears and rubbed her huge belly. We spread her birthing blanket to assure her comfort. Breanna prepared her nesting area. I monitored her every move. Our mother to be was treated like royalty.

The second stage of labor was in full force. My daughter reacted with calmness and intelligence; I was so excited! Anna cleaned herself to prepare her vulva for the first sack dismissal; introducing puppy number one. She opened the sack, licked her baby to greet and clean it and moved the pup towards Breanna. I petted her sides and spoke to her in a very loving tone. Our mommy was doing great.

A brief time passed. Anna altered her position to get more comfortable. Who was next? Puppy two was huge. This one had to hurt coming out, ouch!

Birthing the larger puppy required a longer break between deliveries. Anna rested for a bit. She attended to her two puppies with licks of love. Breanna massaged them to encourage circulation and movement. I recorded their birthing times, weights, and appearances. The three of us made a great team.

Puppy number three was on her way. She was tiny. Anna pulled her out and placed the sack on Breanna's lap. Bre opened the sack and greeted her with a big smile. God couldn't make moments sweeter than this one.

The clock kept ticking; hello puppy four. This pup was a medium golden tone. What will we name this little gentleman? He was spirited, just like his daddy.

Breanna got another gift; our tired mommy removed sack five and passed it right to her midwife. Wow, this was one big boy. He came out growling. Anna swiped that little growl off with one big lick. Mommy rules, puppy drools.

Were we done? No way! Puppy six was a cutie. This little love bug was a light cream color; just beautiful. She evened out the score, three boys to three girls.

Anna took another break. She needed a well-deserved nap. Her little angels were suckling as though they hadn't eaten in a week; now how could that be, they were just born.

Breanna missed puppy seven. I guess someone else dozed off for a minute or two. Anna shocked her when she scooted two pups over to Breanna for babysitting. She was making room for one last miracle.

Yes, it's a girl; the girls won. There were five gorgeous girls and three handsome boys. Say hi to puppy number eight. She was adorable. My goodness, she looked just like her mommy. This mother –-daughter duo were sure to win the mother – daughter lookalike contest of the year.

Breanna and I were sure to recount our pups, double check their genders, retake weights, mark features, and record their birth certificates. We completed our official jobs, "all work and no play", no way. Anna, may we please hold the puppies?

Anna was very comfortable with us; she knew we loved her and her babies dearly. This experience was truly "a golden opportunity". Breanna and I spoke softly, petted gently, and bid the new family a goodnight.

We all needed to get a good night's rest; after all, the work had just begun! Litter maintenance is an eight-week process. We must monitor growth stages, record pup statistics, screen potential buyers, and prepare pup relocation. Remember, a pup sold is never forgotten; pups are a lifelong treasure. Caring for Anna and eight puppies would be "labor of love".

Chapter 5

Growth Stages

Growth and stage development are truly fascinating subjects of discussion. Research for this book has designated a collaboration of materials which have proven to be drawn from superior resources: American Kennel Club literature, "Animal Digest", Pet Wave, as well as multiple veterinarian interviews. These sources list the stages as the following: puppy, (newborn, littermate, eight week, nine weeks, four months to one year also referred to as teenage period), young adulthood, adulthood, and senior adulthood. Please enjoy a breakdown of these stages throughout the paragraphs to follow.

"It's puppy love". Puppies are an exciting challenge. Golden retriever mothers are very proud and dedicated to their litters. Newborn pups are dependent upon their mothers for all of their natural necessities: food, warmth, security, and grooming.

Four weeks is a very inquisitive stage for pups. They begin noticing their whelping box, new scents, and unfamiliar sounds. Maternal disciplining begins with this stage. Litter mates become very helpful, great substitutes during mom's temporary absence. This is a wonderful time to introduce friendly handling; however, one must be cautious and gentle with the pups. Four-week-old pups must remain with their mothers and litters: premature removal of a pup from the litter or mother may result in an emotionally disturbed pup. For example, pups suffering premature removal may develop aggression issues, excessive shyness, and/or behavioral management disorders. Many breeders throughout America truly believe that the end of the seventh week leading into the eighth week as a very emotionally and physically healthy time to introduce and place a pup into a new home.

Pups of eight weeks of age remain very maternally attached; however, begin investigating their exterior environment. They seek the attention of humans; it is the beginning of a very playful and attentive yearning, one which typically continues throughout the life of a golden. This stage is usually predetermined as the most appropriate sale period; however, being that it is also the time from during which the pups deal with fear management, medical specialists urge breeders to wait for the ninth week before promoting relocation or rehousing the pups. A special tip for associating a pup in this stage is to gently roll the pup over for a family belly rub; this pampering shows the pup that it is safe and loved although it is in a submissive position. The pup will learn to adore this technique. Association techniques may be advanced by accompanying the family belly rub with additional play time and petting sessions; therefore, working towards nurturing a healthy and happy dog.

Nine weeks is a wonderful stage for a pup. The pup has developed a stronger sense of security and healthier stability. Trainers are sure to begin the first steps of puppy training during this time period. Loving reinforcement is a great training method during this age. A high pitched voice works best when calling their names. Fear situations should not be coddled, as it may teach the pup that their fearful reaction is appropriate; it is healthier to discourage the scared reaction and assist them to face or cope with the cause of the fear.

Pups ranging eight to fourteen months are a very interesting challenge for owners, trainers, and other household pets. Pups may be labeled rebellious teens; please feel free to compare a pup of this age to a human teenager, notice any similarities? This stage requires strict yet loving discipline, firm consistency, repetitive training, dedicated attention, and incredible patience.

Human family life is a complex network of chaotic rules and changing regulations. For example, a pup may be allowed to sit on the older sofa located in the play room, but not be allowed to sit on the formal sofa located in the living room; take a moment to think like a pup, why is one sofa okay, but not both? The pup cannot separate the identity of the situations; therefore, the rule is too complex for the pup. A second example may be the rule regarding barking, an excited pup may bark when wrestling or playing with a litter mate or play human. Owners may discipline the pup by commanding "no bark". Company may enter the front door, the result being a barking pup. The pup will be allowed to bark as a signal of new people, but then be calmed, an action of discipline, but much softer than a harsh command. The active pup will not understand the action versus reaction of the owner. The pup's ability to cope and learn is determined by their ability to develop human integration, bonding, and association. The quicker a pup develops a means or method of accepting and acknowledging human training, the more skills the pup will adapt. A key training or management tip for this stage of growth is to enforce simplicity, consistency, and positivity. Remember, the human is the boss. Do not allow the pup to take charge. For example, the owner or human should walk through a doorway before the pup. The owner or human should walk up the stairway before the pup, unless specific service skills are required, a pup should not be allowed to charge up the stairs and look down at their owner; this act shows the pup who is the boss. Praise a pup for good behavior; positive reinforcement shows the pup that it is recognized with love and that the human controls knowledge of the behavior. Growing and learning with your pup is a remarkable adventure.

Young adulthood is an incredibly exciting stage. Golden retrievers may be considered young adults at the age of three years. Three-year-olds become a bit more serious. Territorial protectiveness is a sure sign of a pup reaching this stage. Goldens enjoy a playful disposition, active demeanor, and skillful intellect. This stage ranges from age three to age five; however, medical specialists state that adult ranging is not age specific, only approximate.

Training and placement for designated arenas are more defined and implemented at this time. Trainers and owners conduct personality and physical examinations and tests to determine the appropriate role for the golden. Arena specification may be predetermined before purchasing a pup; these scenarios require training modifications and typesetting of goldens' family lineage. Goldens placed in formal arenas such as: service, therapy, military, hunt, police, commercial, show, and search and rescue must dedicate a great deal of their time to training throughout this stage of life. Successful training will promote the dog into a more prominent adulthood.

Goldens truly enjoy adulthood, ages 6-8. Role modeling or career performance is in full swing throughout this stage. Owners are urged to respect appropriate dietary standards. Sufficient exercise schedules assist in the promotion of a healthier life. Please visit your family veterinarian for a complete guide to your dog's health regiment.

Senior adulthood may cover ages 9 to death. Golden retrievers may enjoy a life span of approximately 10 to 12 years; please note the average life span is 11 years old; however, miracle dogs have been fortunate to live a remarkable 14 years. Seniors enjoy family life; a well-deserved retirement from the goldens once successful arena. What a wonderful life!

Personal Reflection

"Our Fierce Hunter"

My husband's true calling in life is hunt training our golden retrievers. He works diligently with the dogs to perfect their skills and passion for the hunting arena. Our females, Abby and Anna, are excellent hunters; proud to serve as superior master hunting tools to their hunter. Readers familiar with hunting dogs have a deep connection with my husband regarding the "hunting drive" concept.

Alex, on the other hand, received his hunt training from a different source, Tilly, our cat. Can you guess what they love to hunt? You have guessed it, mice. There's no mouse in our house!

Luckily, our house does not serve as their hunting ground. Unfortunately, our garage is their targeted land. Having just rebuilt from a house fire, our garage is booming with mice drawn from the construction site, damaged ruins, and multiple donations. This combination has made the garage, mouse heaven, a.k.a. Alex and Tilly's playground.

We are very grateful for all the aid granted us throughout our tragedy; please do not think we were anything less than extremely appreciative. Our issues dealt with the mess created by the house construction and the horrific destruction of items we attempted to salvage. Our garage became the obvious place to hide, sort, and organize all this mess.

Having nowhere to go, our garage became our home sweet home for a few days. Our fire took place on October 18th, 2011, a very chilly day. Our family had been residents of the area for a brief time; we had no close relatives or friends to reach out to, or so we thought. My husband purchased heaters; the mice really appreciated our thoughtfulness. A few quick revisions and the garage was turned into a respectful living quarters. We set up a living room, a few beds for the kids, and rented a port-a-potty. Who could ask for anything more, all of us! Thank God for the kindness of great neighbors. Barb and Jim saved us. They welcomed our entire family, six of us, into their home. Our community extended their loving hands; we were offered a rental home from the Baptist Church. New Life Church congregation welcomed us with love, respect, and donations to fill our empty lives. God taught us, all bad things happen for good reasons. Our daughter, Maranda remarked, "Ya know mom, our old house was in bad shape and you and daddy have been working a lot just to fix stuff. The new house will not need all the fixing, so you and daddy can spend more time with us". It was a harsh lesson, but a true one. Our family and friends worked hard as a team to rebuild our world.

The hardest part of this tragedy was that our dogs were not allowed at our gifted rental. My husband and I sadly respected the rules but had a serious time with its strict requirements. Our dogs were our family. Our dear friend, Lonnie, our kids, and my husband and I rotated caring for the dogs. We spent as much time as we could with them. The garage served as their temporary home away from home. This was the time period Alex grew to love hunting mice.

Our family and friends dedicated a great deal of time to caring for our dogs, but they were still faced with some alone time. What's that old saying, "the cat's away so the mice will play"? Goldens are naturally very spirited and playful. Alex's new game, this golden is the new cat in the hat. Please allow us to mention, our kitten, Skittles died in our fire. She is dearly loved and missed. Alex attempted to take over her job. He highly respected her previous work but was definitely no replacement for her talented craftiness as a skilled mouse hunter. Everyone laughed at his hunting excursions. The mice were quick to realize that he was no match for them. They began teasing him. Our foolish pup just couldn't get it; he stalks the mouse, sneaks up quietly, prepares to jump on it and "Bash, Bang, Boom" knocks over everything in his pathway! The mice were kind enough to make sure he hadn't hurt himself as they waved goodbye. It became obvious, Alex needed hunt training.

Tilly, our new kitten, to the rescue. This little kitten had it going on. She had the moves; above all, she welcomed teaching her new pal, Big Al, how to get the job done right. The two of them make quite a pair; a much better match than Alex and the black bear; or were they?

Lesson one, watch and learn. Tilly showed Alex her famous sneak attack maneuvers. He would practice for hours. Boy those two shared long naps. She quickly realized anything in Al's way would get destroyed. This smart cat thought out a plan of action, if he couldn't work around the junk, move it out of his way. This was the beginning of Alex's new career, exterior decorating; a.k.a. cleaning out our garage.

Move it or destroy it, Big Al's policy towards his becoming a master mouser. He worked hard to maneuver anything that got in his way, out of his way. The big brat would sneak into our garage; by the way, did we mention that it is a six-car garage? Thinking we'd allowed him outside to enjoy the fresh air, playing in the woods, or goofing around with our other goldens, we didn't expect him of any crime. Wrong, wrong, very wrong! Our once clean front yard had been decorated with garbage, donations, and collectables, our personal belongings versus Alex's removable treasures. What an eye sore. We were not happy golden owners.

Parents make mistakes; we are not perfect. We blamed the kids; after all, our gorgeous show, commercial, breeding, and therapy golden couldn't have, wouldn't have, done something like this. The kids had alibis. The kitten had been evicted to living in the basement with no chance of parole. There was nobody left to blame; it had to be our big baby, "Alamonster". How could he do this to us? Easy answer, it was fun!

The smarty pants figured it out, ok, let's be honest, he watched Tilly. The more things he moved out of his way, the better chance he had at catching the mice. It worked; he got better and better at both careers: exterior decorating and mouse hunting.

Alex was so happy when our garage lock was broken. This granted him free access into the garage. He would play in there for hours, or shall we say out there, he'd walk in to pick up an item that was in his pathway and place it anywhere outside that was out of his way. Once he had removed what bothered him, he'd attack. The mouse count quickly deteriorated. He wanted to show off his kills of the day; we were blessed to discover his little pile of dead mice on our front porch at the end of each day. YUCK!

The kids and I weren't his willing workers; he made the mess, but we had to clean it up. No fair, I was with the kids on this one. We had our roles: Bre put toothpaste in his mouth, mouse breath, pu, Maranda, Brian, and Mikey picked up the garbage and belongings he had distributed in our yard. I searched for a new lock.

There was no stopping him, or was there. Bruce to the rescue; he bought a new lock on his drive home from work. Alex wasn't too happy.

We crack up laughing over seeing Alex standing by the garage door. He uses his front paw and knocks on the door. "There's no one home", laugh the little mice. Does this scenario remind anyone of the three little pigs and big bad wolf?

Don't forget about Alex's second career, exterior decorating. We got him an application at the city dump. Hey, can he use you for a reference?

Chapter 6
Character Description

Temperament is a vital subject regardless of developmental stage. A loving, loyal, gentle disposition is the trademark of the golden retriever. "Happy go lucky" a popular cliché warmly identifying the trustworthy breed serves as a breed marker in numerous hunting clubs. Professional breeders and medical specialists will state that a goldens name is derived from their coat color; however, a loving pet owner may demand it is based on their golden temperament.

There are exceptions to the "golden rule". Breeding goldens will exhibit aggressive behavior during heat, pregnancy, and motherhood. Pups coping with premature displacement may portray aggressive behaviors. Goldens dealing with an abusive history are known for aggression disorders. Selective situations or medical disorders may step in to create aggression problems. Professional trainers handle aggression matters with cautious skill and careful sensitivity. Please note the paragraphs to follow for further discussion.

There are different forms of dog aggression. Dog aggression may be categorized as: inter-dog or dog-on-dog, handler-to-dog, dominant, fear/defense, and territorial. Aggression management is based on the type of aggression.

Inter-dog aggression usually occurs between same sex dogs. The warning signs include hair raising, growling, lunging, snarling, staring, and challenged attacks. Female on female attacks are typically much more serious; bitches have been known to fight to their death. Male on male aggression is noted for one male submitting: therefore surrendering dominance. Dog fights are powered by an adrenaline drive known as, "blind rage".

Training methods regarding inner-dog aggression may refer to training methods entitled: B.A.T., C.A.T., and multiple reward based methods. Please note this scenario. Place a helper non-aggressive dog at a pin pointed location. Lead the aggressive dog on secured lead towards the helping dog. Stop at the point or distance at which the aggressive dog becomes stressed. Wait for the aggressive dog to show an indication of calm behavior: smelling the ground, turning away from the helping dog, or resting in place; then move the aggressive dog away and treat the dog for a positive reaction. Repeating this activity should progress to the aggressive dog and helping dog becoming united. A second method is entitled, constructional aggression treatment. Place a helping dog to a designated point; allow the dog to relax as it awaits the arrival of the aggressive dog. The trainer may bring the aggressive dog into the scenario; the trainer may relax, simply monitoring the dogs. A second assistant would remove or relocate the aggressive dog, taking it to a location farther away until the dog has reached its comfort zone. Once this distance and time range has been achieved, a reapproach may be attempted. Repetition of this activity should prove to calm the aggressive behavior; thus marking the exercise as successful. A third method is to work with treat reward systems. Please follow this scenario; step one: make sure the dog is hungry, step two: place the dog on a strong lead, locate your aggressive dog at a designated sight, step three: have a helping dog approach the aggressive dog, step four: give the aggressive dog a treat the moment it sees the helping dog, step five: allow the helping dog to stay at the sight unless the aggressive dog shows an act of aggression, step six: remove the helping dog at point or indication of aggression, step seven: reapproach with the helping dog, step eight: give the aggressive dog a treat at the first sight of the helping dog, and step nine is to repeat this act until the aggressive dog realizes that the presence of the helping dog is a positive act resulting in a reward; therefore the aggressive dog stops its aggressive action or behavior. Repetition is the key to achieving lasting success.

Handler versus dog aggression is much rarer. Dogs instinctively like people. Human versus dog aggression may occur in the following cases: a person may be injured as a result of an attempt to break up an inter-dog fight, an individual may be harmed in cases of protection, abused dogs grow weary of humans, dogs suffering malnutrition, a form of abuse, may become aggressive towards the human, and professional arena dogs: military, police, and guard may be forced to assert aggression as part of their arena requirement. Our research did not uncover any handler versus dog aggression reports which were not categorized within the previous list above.

Trainers state that the primary solution for handler verses dog aggression is the provision of love and care for the dog; thus eliminating issues of abuse, the leading cause of handler verses dog aggression. Self-protection, removing oneself from an inter-dog aggressive act, is highly recommended; obviously an individual cannot be harmed if he or she is not in harm's way. Training tools such as harnesses, protective collars and fences assist in preventing or stopping handler versus dog acts of aggression.

Dominance aggression is described as the dog fearing being dominated or refusing to submit to acts of dominance. It is noted in households, where the pet may have issues with excessive punishment or discipline, a reaction to pronounced staring, a sharp reaction to the removal of personal property such as a dog toy and yet many other scenarios. Signs of this form of aggression include, but are not limited to: snarling, growling, biting, forward stance, and baring teeth. Dominance aggression is not common in golden retrievers.

Treatment and training programs have developed successful methods of coping with this form of aggression. Trainers extend their skillful hand to the human; teaching the human to express loving respect, rather than sharp discipline has proven highly successful. Reducing the level of dominance shown in the dog creates a decrease of dominance from the dog. Love goes a long way with a golden retriever. Talking in a firm voice is much more productive than yelling or hitting. Respecting body language or body

signaling is a wonderful method of training or treating the dog. Owners may gently wake their golden; an owner may call their dog's name a few times, and then softly nudge the dog; this wake up is much nicer than pushing the dog off of a bed. Dogs dislike dominant signals: reaching over the dog, quick movements towards the dog's food or toys, and loud harsh voices. Lower the vocal volume, talk don't yell; yelling becomes distorted, making it difficult for the dog to understand the commands. Summing up the perfect treatment for this aggression disorder, share a mutual respect between humans and dogs.

Fearful aggression also known as defensive aggression occurs in cases when a dog believes it is in a threatening situation and has no or slight escape. The dog may be reacting normally or in a healthy manner based on its predicament. Fear aggression is more common at about twelve weeks of age and again at the time of sexual maturity. This form of aggression does not express a gender preference. Fear aggression signals two instinctive acts: fight or flight. Signs of fear aggression may include, but are not limited to trembling, barking, snarling, snapping, growling, cowering, and baring teeth. This form of aggression is highly noted in dogs that are chained or restricted; therefore, cannot run away. Humans suffer the risk of injury from this form because the human who restricted the dog may be called upon to eliminate or alter the form of restriction. Abuse is a leading cause of this aggression disorder. Goldens are rarely affected by this type of aggression.

Treatment recommendations involve three training guides: establishing safety zones, eliminating abusive situations, and providing quality care. Owners must establish appropriate means of restricting their dog. Fencing is a safer means of restricting than is a chain. Chains may limit the dog from searching for trouble, but they do not stop trouble from finding the dog. Dog abuse is wrong; this tragic issue must be treated for the protection and prosperity of the dog. Fear breeds aggression if not handled accordingly. Trainers firmly recommend face fears do not coddle the reaction to the fear or the dog will learn that the reaction earns attention; therefore, their reaction worsens, leading to aggression for attention. Implementing specific training methods may solve or stop this aggressive form.

Territorial aggression may be described as a protective measure taken by the dog to express possessive behavior or guarding skills. Dogs express stronger territorial aggression in scenarios involving boundary protection: houses, cars, property, and so forth. The guarding of favorite toys, food, people and yet defined objects characterize this form of aggression as well. Many owners actually train dogs for territorial aggression as a means of guarding or policing assistance.

Signs of this form may be stated as: snarling, growling, barking, lunging, baring teeth, hair-raising, biting, and attacking an enemy. The dog may express levels of aggression based on what or where it is protecting. For example, though goldens rarely become aggressive, they may show territorial aggression in cases of a crime against their owner, house or property; however, it would be very rare for a golden to show territorial aggression over a toy or food.

Trainers work very hard to conquer this aggression form. A leading treatment recommendation is stranger contact testing. Please follow this scenario; introduce a stranger, a protected individual, onto the property. The dog may react aggressively. The dog trainer or owner should greet the stranger in a friendly manner; this act shows the dog that it is ok for the stranger to be on his or her land. Introduce the dog to the stranger in a cheerful voice. The dog should quickly learn that it is a positive situation and not express any aggression toward the visitor. Repeat this act using the same person for a few trials and later alternating strangers. A treat may be offered by the owner once it is clear that the dog is not expressing aggression. Please research additional training methods for assistance.

Qualified trainers should be referenced for all forms of aggression disorders. Safety is a must in all situations. Please contact your chosen medical expert and/or professional trainer for advice and assistance.

Personal Reflection

"Free Fun"

Family fun is very important to us. We are always searching for new ideas for fun activities at a great price. Our budget being tight and squeaky, we were on the hunt for free fun for everyone.

Let's share some ideas. Seriously, write to us with suggestions. We love trying new things. Would you like to hear this "Freebee Fun Blaster"?

Reminisce a little; have you ever played dress up? We sure did as kids. What's good enough for the parent is good enough for the kids. Who is trying on who's what? What is that thing, who looks like who? Who put that on which golden? What a laugh!

We called a family meeting. Bruce and I asked each person to clean out their dressers and closets. Everyone was to bring us items that were too small, torn, stained or disliked. We thought, what a better way to do spring cleaning. Once we had completed our gathering, we tossed everything on a huge pile. This game had just begun.

The first part of the game was for each person to choose three items out of the pile and try them on. More items could be selected, once each person had a chance to pick the first three. Individuals could return items if they could not wear them. Items went flying in the air. Everyone was tossing, switching, and laughing. This was super free fun!

Watching the kids' imaginations was cool. They were so curious. Breanna just had to get Alex involved. He loves "showing off". She put a baseball jersey on him. Maranda, our girly girl, tried a pretty dress on Abby; remember, Abby is our master hunter; who goes hunting in a pink dress? Brian and Mikey found Maranda's old tutu; check out Anna; isn't she beautiful? The kids had more fun putting the clothes on our goldens than on one another. The dogs had a blast as well. Come on, tell us your kids have never dressed up your pet. We thought so.

Let's keep laughing. We instructed the kids to return all items to the pile. It was time to add a twist to this game. We blind folded the kids. The dogs were good; they got to see what was coming. We told the kids they were allowed to choose four items out of the pile and dress one dog. Adding to the mix, we paired Breanna with Anna, Maranda with Alex, and the boys with Abby. Ready, set go . . . the race was on. We aren't stupid parents; what did the kids think, we weren't born yesterday; yeah, we knew they were peeking! The question was, who is going for which look? Will Maranda attempt to be handsome? Do the boys appreciate Abby's favorite job? What would Anna like to wear to the party? This was so funny. The clock was ticking; no peeking, right! Okay, let's check out our contestants.

Introducing Miss Anna, escorted by Miss Breanna. She was wearing a sassy t- shirt and blue skirt. Those girls were cute. Say hello to Miss Abby; she proudly entered the room with her young men. These handsome hunks dressed our hunting girl in a pink camouflage shirt and jean shorts; Abby wasn't too sure about the pink, but at least it was hunter camouflage. Alexander was a proud peacock; hosting his little lady, Miss Maranda; the two show offs looked sharp as a whip in their bridal attire. All in all, "looking good".

We gathered all the items and bagged them for Good Will. We'd had our family fun, now it was time to turn the items over to someone else who was in need. Having accomplished our spring clean-up and enjoyed a few laughs, it was time to go shopping for new ideas.

CHAPTER 7
Grooming Techniques

Grooming is a wonderfully interesting health subject. Goldens wear a gorgeous coat, requiring quality love and care grooming techniques. A well-groomed golden demands care in the following categories: hair, cleanliness, ears, nails, and dental.

Groomers will implement the use of specific instruments designated for coat regions and appearance requirements. Owners and groomers may fancy a grooming kit with the following items: fine tooth comb, soft bristle brush, hard wire bristle brush, blow dryer (cold and warm air capability), grooming table, flat tipped scissors, mirrors, and lighting equipment. These tools must be implemented by a master trained groomer or a loving well trained owner/ handler.

Hair maintenance of a golden retriever will differ based on the role of the dog. For example working arenas such as: commercial, show, therapy, and service goldens take great pride in their presentation; a gorgeous appearance is vital in their career roles. Preparing a show dog for the ring requires special care: a fine tooth comb may provide a streaming affect when feathering the dogs hind quarter hair, a soft bristle brush may be implemented when attempting to decrease frizz or static, a wire brush works well for removing snarls, a flat protective scissors may be needed to snip a snarl or two, not one speck of dirt may be captured in a show ring, a quick bath calls for a blow dryer and the right lighting equipment exposes every hair out of place; quick check out the mirror for a last minute review before walking down that runway to success.

Regardless of their chosen arena, all goldens enjoy a little pampering every now and then, who likes a bad hair day! Golden retrievers are known for excessive shedding; especially in spring and winter; therefore, a daily brushing routine is a must for all goldens. Goldens are very social dogs; most love getting beautified for a day out in society. Performing healthy grooming techniques assists in great health maintenance; a well-groomed dog is a healthy dog.

Splish splash, ready for your golden's bath! Scrub a dub dub, prepare that tub; a golden should be bathed once a month, more frequent bathing may be required for more active or public goldens as they do carry a distinctive body odor. No, jumping in the lake does not fulfill bathing requirements. Yes, a quality dog shampoo is preferred. The dos and don'ts of bathing may be designated by the role of the golden.

"Hello, can you hear me?" Ear care is vital for a golden. Cleansing with veterinarian approved solutions is maintenance must.

Nail care is required for those goldens who do not naturally wear down their own nails. Many goldens who walk on cement or strong surfaces wear or grind their nails naturally; however, those who do not come into frequent contact with such surfaces require nail care to prevent scratching, tearing and breakage. Nail care is a lifelong issue.

The subject of dewclaw removal faces controversy. Professionals carry serious arguments on both sides. Many feel the dewclaws should not be removed because the dog carries a line of protective immunity within the dewclaw. Experts also feel it is dangerous to allow the dog to keep the dewclaw because of accidental tearing. Dewclaw removal is partially based on which arena the dog is enrolled. Show and commercial dogs are split down the middle; some handlers select removal and others feel it is unnecessary. Hunting and search and rescue dogs are prominent candidates for dewclaw removal. The additional arenas indicate large variations in choice. This choice remains the decision of the breeder but should be taken under educated consideration. Monitoring the nails is a safety procedure all owners, groomers, handlers, and health care professionals should respect.

Want a big sloppy kiss? Before you pucker up, make sure your golden has enjoyed its weekly tooth brushing. Appropriate dental care prevents tooth decay, oral odors, and gum disease. Goldens will adapt to tooth brushing by repeating this activity on a strict schedule. Dietary care provides healthy protection for a golden retriever's teeth. Selecting correct foods and treats is a process requiring appropriate dietary education. Let's see that gorgeous smile!

Please conduct personal research for further information or additional suggestions. Your goldens grooming necessities are vital to their health and happiness.

Personal Reflection

"Grin and Bear It"

Our home is in a heavily wooded area. Having moved here recently, we had a lot to learn about our new environment. Lesson one; living in the woods is very different than a city park with a lot of trees.

Woods provide housing for many wild animals. We were amazed by the wonder of the great outdoors; gorgeous deer, beautiful birds, silly squirrels, and of course bouncing bunnies. Shock set in, with the realization of a few other roommates: coyotes, wolves, and bears. Don't these animals belong in a zoo, for goodness sake!

The kids and I had to take protective steps. Safety and sensibility had to go hand in hand if we were going to make this living situation work. The kids were instructed to stay in our immediate yard unless an adult was accompanying them. No one was allowed out alone after dark. Rule by rule, we could handle things; after all, we had our goldens for protection and companionship.

Have we mentioned, goldens do not make great protectors; they are like big teddy bears, ha ha; therefore, they score big as wonderful companions.

Forest friends make great new pals. Abby's love of bunnies has been discussed. Anna thinks the world of a lively squirrel; great exercise, chase a squirrel for an hour. Alexander, now just who do you think he chose to befriend?

The King of the show arena has to play with the King of the forest. Round one, baby black bear versus young adult golden retriever. Would anyone like to guess the outcome?

What would a baby black bear and a young golden have in common? They both like water, food and wrestling. Screams filled the air! We rushed out to see what was wrong. Michael was running as fast as he could. "Mom, Mom, Alex is swimming with a bear". My first thought, "Great four year old imagination". He grabbed my hand and pulled me all the way down to our pond. Oh my heavens, he was right. It was precious, that was for a minute. Terror set in, when we saw the mama bear racing towards the pond. I told Michael to get to the house as fast as he could. I called Alex out of the pond; of course, why listen to mom on a hot day, swimming outweighs any command. He finally moved his butt when he caught a look at one mad mama bear. We rushed our scared butts back to the house; should I admit my great golden protector was about fifty feet in front of my slow moving behind. Luckily, mama and baby were more interested in a swim, than mauling us. Splish splash, who's taking a bath?

Our gorgeous show dog needed a real bath and grooming session. He loves water, that is, unless it involves the use of soap. Breanna and I prepared his tub, called him in for his bath and hid all the soap containers. Alex proudly stepped into the tub. Great start, he played with his rubber duck, pushed his little boat around and never noticed Breanna applying the shampoo. Scrub a dub dub, this fool likes his tub.

Tricking him into taking a bath was easy; does anyone have any ideas for convincing him that the blow dryer is not his worst enemy? Breanna manned the blow dryer, while I combed, brushed, trimmed and fluffed his gorgeous hair. One, two, three hours, that was hours of grooming to produce a master show dog. I wish someone would pamper me!

Big Al liked to eat alone. We would make up the dog dishes set them out in a line for the goldens to share and then prepare our own dinner. We found this worked great, no dogs begging for human food. Alex had his own dinner plan; pick up his dish, take it outside, lay in the shade, and dine.

Dine alone, well, that's just rude. Why dine alone, invite a very hungry guest. Bears love dog chow, a lot, but so does Big Al. Remember, he took his dish outside to dine alone for a reason; he doesn't like sharing. Growl to growl, the battle was raging. Paws up, they were ready to duke it out. The first blow shot through the air. "Blast, Boom, Bang! It wasn't good. The bear was on the run, toting his reward, Alex's food. The crime scene was a horrific sight, blood everywhere.

Our precious Alex was close to death. Oh my God, what do we do? Prayers rushed into our heads. Please dear God, save our love bug.

We contacted our vet; get him here fast was all we needed to hear. My daughter held him in our car. He was trembling with pain; she was shaking with worry. Our dear friend, Steve was driving faster than a jet could fly. The vet met us at the door. Hurry up and wait, the magic of medicine, please let Doc save our big baby. The clock ticked and tocked; finally, we heard footsteps coming our way. Did we want to hear the news? Would it be bad, good, or the worst? Thank goodness for that soft smile on our vet's face. Alex would be ok.

Alex had a huge hole in his side. The tear in his side was from the sweep of the bear's paw. The wound was deep and wide. It could not be stitched. We had to irrigate the wound three times a day to flush the germs from dirt particles and hair follicles. This care process was a true act of love; especially, on behalf of my son, Mikey and daughter, Breanna. They took great care of their King baby; spoiling him every day. We were sure he was healed, but he put on quite an act to trick a little more attention out of his little doctor and nurse. Friends or enemies, black bears and golden retrievers do not work in a relationship.

Chapter 8

Training Methods

Training a dog is a must in developing a healthy and happy life shared by a dog and owner. Dog training is an ongoing process throughout the life span of the dog. Three points establish training formats: life stages, arena placement, and necessity requirements. Once the reason for training has been determined, the type of trainer and training method can be selected.

Puppies require many types of training throughout the stages of puppy life. Stage of development designates the core of all training decisions. Newborn pups require socializing. Pups begin life with their mom and littermates. The litter owner is prompted to begin touching and talking to the newborns at approximately three weeks of age. Pups enjoy human touch; a gentle belly rub, little ear scratch, few kind words and holding the pup close to a loving body means a great deal in the positive development of a dog's personality. Socialization training, the personal contact shared between a human and pup/dog, continues throughout the pup's/dog's life span. A pup requires more contact as it grows; professionals strongly urge multiple people share in the contact schedules, commonly called playtime. Human to dog socialization is healthy for both the human, as well as the dog.

Please allow us to implement our personal reference at this time. Being private breeders, we have researched and experienced puppy life throughout the past fifteen years. Puppy socialization is one of the most enjoyable parts of being a breeder and dog lover.

Research has taught us a great deal regarding the tremendous differences in socialization styles amongst breeders. Professional breeding programs or kennel businesses handle socialization with a different format than private breeders. Professional breeders and kennel breeders may employ staffs who are assigned to provide quality care provision for the litters. The employee may be scheduled to clean kennels or cages, exercise pups and provide nutritional measures. It is during this care assignment that the staff member may be allotted a brief time to play with the pups. The employee has but a short time to communicate, (talk, touch and show affection) with the pup on a social scale.

Private breeders relate to the subject of socialization on a different page. Pups born to a private breeder are usually a welcomed resident of the family household. The pups are exposed to family activities, as a typical part of their development. Privately bred pups hear human voices on a more regular basis. Family members casually or freely take time from their life to pet and play with the pups, rather than working this into a care provision schedule. For example, most professional breeders close the day by setting a specific light out time or end of the business day; therefore, the litters are settled for that time. Private breeders, on the other hand, share their home life with the litters. My husband, Bruce, is fond of sleeping with a pup or two; he is worse than our kids. Pups may get noisy; the perfect signal for a family member to take a few minutes to pet them. Life convenience plays it role: it is easier for a family member to enjoy watching a movie as they snuggle a pup, than it may be for an employee to find open time for some additional time for socialization.

We are not stating that private breeders are better than professional breeders, only different. Pups begin their socialization during this early pup stage; however, it is a continual life process, which passes to the pup's new owners. Regardless of which breeding format the pup is exposed to, having enjoyed a healthy start, the pup has a wonderful chance to live a happy life with their new family.

It's a brand new world; welcome to the pup's new home. Pups may endure a number of fears: sounds, people, locations, and other pets. Socialization plays a key role in fear management. Introducing new things in an appropriate manner is very important. The second step in fear management is training the pup to handle the fear in a positive manner. Socialization training will implement the combination of fear introduction and management to nurture a healthy pup.

Behavioral training is very important to older dogs as well as puppies. Owners should be educated as to the rights and wrongs with canine behavior. Subjects which should be addressed may include, but are not limited to: chewing, barking, socializing, cowering and pottying. Behavioral training begins with one basic point; diagnose the cause of the behavior and eliminate or manage the cause. Owners should ask themselves the big question; why did my golden retriever do that behavior? Asking the question leads to finding the correct answer.

Allow us to address some specific behaviors that owners cope with on a regular basis. Chewing is a major behavioral issue. Dogs naturally chew. The dog chews as a means of release; it is a wonderful stress release. Chewing is an act of nature; dogs must eat, so obviously they must chew their food. Destructive chewing may be a problem. Why would a dog chew in a destructive manner? One reason may be dental problems. Dogs will chew to force a loose tooth to break free; what better to chew on than the owner's new shoe. Problem chewing may occur as a struggle for attention. Owners will pay a great deal of attention to the dog that ruined their favorite table. Kids get busy, sometimes too busy to play with their dog; a kid will pay attention to a dog who has just chewed up their favorite toy. Remove the cause of the negative chewing; encourage the positive chewing, as it is a matter of good health. For example, remember to take more time out for a belly rub, ear scratch, and game of fetch; it may save that new shoe. Dental checkups are important; monitor the dog's teeth for troubles; it is easier than awaiting the dog chewing to pull out its own tooth. Supplying an adequate amount of healthy chewies will prevent negative chewing situations. The training method is obvious, remove the negative cause and produce a positive outcome.

Barking is one of the most irritating negative behaviors. Why is the dog barking? Good question. Determine the cause and eliminate the problem.

Barking is not always a negative issue. Watch, guard, police, and military dogs bark as a means of signaling and protecting. These dogs are trained as to when and how to bark. These dogs are definitely not the norm.

Typical barking situations may call for limited barking. Is the dog barking at company? Did a car beep, all dogs would bark over that sound. Sounds unusual to the environment create a stress for the dog; therefore, the dog reacts by barking. The dog should bark, after all, it is an act of nature. It is not the act of barking that creates the problem; it is the abundance of barking that develops the issue.

Uncontrollable barking is annoying. A dog should quiet upon command. Dogs are smart; they can control their bark, but may choose to overreact. Extensive barking may be a result of: craving attention, excessive boredom, prolonged irritability and ill health. Please note the following scenarios.

Dogs may bark at someone they dislike. Two methods of treatment or training may be implemented to solve this issue. Requesting the person in question to leave the vicinity would stop the dog barking. This may appear drastic; however, many professionals will stand strong in the belief that a dog is a powerful judge of character; therefore, the person must be a negative person for the dog to react in a negative manner. One problem we personally have with this method is that we are concerned that the dog will continue negative behavior thinking that it has the upper hand; the dog will learn that it was superior over the human; thus placing it as pack leader, rather than the human being the leader. This situation must be governed with great caution; it may be effective if the dog owner maintains leader position over the dog, though the disliked human has submitted the position. The second suggestion is to socialize the dog and disliked individual. Work on forming a healthier relationship between the two parties. Reintroduce the person and dog using reward therapy. Secure the irritated dog in its crate. Have the disliked person sit near the crate and talk to the dog in a cheerful voice for a few minutes. If the dog appears calm and positive, open the crate. Allow the dog to choose when or if it is going to come out of its secure crate. The disliked person may toss a treat to the dog, a peace offering. The disliked person and owner should engage in a cheerful conversation, showing the dog that the situation is healthy. Time allotted, proof of a positive human to human relationship, and positive reinforcement may lead to the disliked person becoming the liked person.

Dogs present negative behavior: uncontrollable barking, excessive whining, or inappropriate toileting as a reaction to negative situations. Removing the cause is the first solution to these issues. Life does not always grant dog owners that option. The second method for dealing with negative behaviors is an act of socializing the dog to accept the cause of the behavior. For example, owners dealing with dogs who have storm issues cannot remove the cause; only Mother Nature can step into those shoes. Training the dog to accept the situation it must deal with is a matter of socializing the dog to the cause.

Please accept our personal training suggestion regarding storm scenarios. We recommend introducing noises at early stages of life. The use of storm recordings is very helpful; simply play the recorded storm at a reasonable level for the pup's to grow familiar with the sounds. Placing the pup or dog in its crate during a storm with its favorite toys and chewies reduces its anxiety. Playing moderate to somewhat loud music from time to time also introduces additional sounds which will reduce the dog's anxiety during a storm. Thanks to modern technology it is also recommended to implement the use of storm simulators which will introduce the sound effects, thus building up healthier tolerance. Obviously, the use of musical technology and storm simulators cannot produce the same environmental impact, but these methods can make a significant difference in the dog's emotional tolerance of the storm. Once the dog is more comfortable and familiarized to the situations, the dog will reduce the negative behavior; or in other words, socialization training has been successful.

There are numerous behaviors to be discussed. The training is the same for all behaviors. Remove or alter the negative cause. Once the negative cause has been controlled, the negative behavior will be stopped.

Encouraging positive behavior requires positive training techniques. Dogs will learn healthy behavior from positive reinforcement and positive training. Providing quality attention, positive attitudes, and healthy intellect when gearing towards promoting healthy behaviors will increase learning capabilities.

One training example may be taken from training hearing impaired service dogs. The dog is trained to react to an alarm sounding. The service dog's job is to wake the hearing-impaired person when the alarm sounds. Trainers may approach this by using treats. The dog hears the alarm; it then is instructed to nudge the hearing-impaired person. The dog may be given a treat when it awakens the hearing-impaired person. Some trainers actually hide treats by the person; the dog will search for the treat. The person awakens from the dog attempting to find the reward. This creates a positive reaction to the alarm's sound.

A dog barks at the car alarm. The owner should not discipline the dog for barking, rather for not stopping. This may be done by using positive reinforcement. The alarm sounds, reaction, barking. The owner states, "No barking". The dog continues barking. The alarm stops, but the dog barks. The owner repeats, "No barking". The dog stops barking. The owner gives the dog a big hug and praises it, "Good dog, no barking". The positive attention will gear the dog to stop barking at a quicker rate, as it realizes that it will get attention for listening.

Please seek more information on behavioral training. It is a massive and wonderful subject.

Socialization training may include: human contact, territorial foundation, pet placement, and environmental association. The most critical stage of socialization is between 3 and 17 weeks of age. Human contact should begin with the litter owner, expand to the care providers or family unit, transfer to the new owner/s and build to a list of additional family and friends. Introducing the pup to new people is vital to their social development. This act should be done in a casual and calm manner, as to reduce the fear factor for the pup.

The role of the pup owner is very important throughout the socialization of a pup into adulthood. Fear management must be highly respected, as it may lead to negative problems if not handled carefully. Owners are urged to remain positive throughout the socialization process. A pup expressing fear is normal; an owner over coddling the scared pup is trouble. A scared pup should receive attention, but in a positive manner. Do not play into the fear; rather, show the pup not to fear or to reduce the cause of the fear. Please note this scenario. The pup may be standing near its owner, welcome a new person into the room, the owner should greet the person with warmth, a smile or polite vocal tone; this shows the pup that the person is safe. The owner may address the pup with a pat on the back; the new person may follow this lead and pet the pup as well. Blending the tone and touch of both people together will reduce or dismiss the pup's fear; therefore develop a positive new relationship between the pup and its new friend.

A valuable note must be introduced at this point. Please monitor the exterior contact allowed for a pup in cases involving health risks. Pups that are not completely health guarded, meaning those who have not had the appropriate vaccinations should not be in contact with situations involving unguarded animals. Health issues may arise due to unsafe exposure. Please seek appropriate medical care for all pups as a preventative measure.

Puppy obedience courses are highly recommended. These programs encourage healthy human to dog socialization, as well as promoting dog to dog socialization. Pups learn their role within the pup/dog world. The time frame 12-16 weeks serves as the most opportune time for pups to enroll in such pup training programs. This time table welcomes personal owner and pup socialization training, in unity with a professional or formal setting.

Modification is the primary rule when socializing the pup. Owners should slowly, but steadily associate their pup to the world. Overwhelming a pup is not healthy. Professionals recommend introducing one new stimulant per day. This allows the pup to adapt to the new person, place, or thing at a calm rate. It is nice to have a day or two each week for the pup and owner to share quality personal time, not every day has to contain something or someone new. Take life one day at a time; remember the saying, "stop and smell the roses" or in dog language, "stop and rub my belly".

Adult dogs require socialization to maintain a healthy life. Golden retrievers adore socializing with humans and other dogs. Dogs enjoy new experiences with ease as they age. Goldens like to enjoy the best of both worlds; they like associating with new dogs and people; meeting new stimulants entertains them. Family attention comforts them and develops a secure feeling of contentment. Balancing both types of social activity will produce a very happy and healthy dog throughout its adulthood.

Senior dogs usually prefer to share more time with immediate family members. They do not dislike external contacts; they simply feel more at ease with those they love. Seniors being somewhat like human elders, favor certain aches and pains; therefore, take fewer risks and interact in more restricted situations as a means of self-protection. Outside stimulants should still be presented, but not as often. It is advised to announce new stimulants, but at a graciously reduced rate. Respect the dog and its age. Capability for socialization may be based on age, acceptance, and alertness.

Crate training is the preference of the owner. Owners vary in opinion regarding crating preferences. The key points when considering crating include, but may not be limited to: schedule, size, and usage. These points are to be taken into great consideration when determining if a crate is an appropriate tool, what type of crate is the best purchase, and what rules will be implemented for the specific situation.

The most valuable notation regarding crating is that the crate must be respected as the pup's/dog's home within their home. It is their private land of contentment and comfort. Measures taken to produce this secure home may include many factors. The size of the crate is very important. Dogs prefer smaller places to snuggle and relax, but appropriate room is required for standing and stretching. The flooring of the crate must be adequate for comfort and health. Owners are urged to alternate a group of toys and chewies for their pet; granting the same toy may result in territorial behavior; thus, alternating them reduces possessiveness. Do not overcrowd the crate; a few selections are just fine, but allow space for the pet itself to be comfortable. Do not allow toileting within the crate; crate extensions are implemented for crate toileting. Crates do reduce damage and toilet accidents; however, remember, ample time must be allowed outside of this crate for healthy life maintenance.

Training a pup or dog to enter and use a crate is actually not as difficult as one may fear. Crate training is easier for a pup, but dogs may be taught new tricks. Owners may trick the pup or dog into entering the crate by using a reward method. Show the treat or toy to the dog/pup; do not allow the dog/pup to take the treat or toy until it has entered the crate. The animal will learn that entering the crate is a positive thing ending in a treat or toy. Owners are prompted to place treats and toys inside of the crate. The dog/pup will discover these items and be greatly pleased with its crate's contents. The time spent inside of the crate will become the dog's/pup's private play time; therefore, the pet will look at crate time with a positive view. Crate time used for punishment should not involve the use of treats or toys; remove all such objects when placing the pet inside of its crate as a punishment. The items may be returned when the punishment time is completed. The dog/pup will learn great respect for their crate.

Potty training is a must when raising a pup. The key points to potty training may be listed as: consistency, repetition, and patience. Owners must determine which style of potty training they prefer; outdoor, indoor, and blend. Outdoor training seriously reduces the amount of pup mess from the home. Owners selecting this method may have an exterior kennel for placement during absent periods. Owners dealing with exterior restrictions and/or extended absent periods may prefer indoor training. Exterior restrictions such as apartment life, lack of outdoor kenneling or fencing, and yard reduction play a valuable role in outdoor capabilities. Those owners coping with extended absents may feel it kinder to implement indoor facilities for the pup's comfort and health. The most popular choice of restricted owners; those coping with residential and time issues is entitled, blend, the combination of indoor and outdoor. Numerous pup and dog owners believe this combination is the best of both worlds; it is a subject of controversy with professionals because of the intellectual requirements of the pup in dealing with divided training rules. The final choice of potty training methods is regulated by the pup's/dog's owner and the lifestyle welcoming the animal.

Scheduling is a vital tool in potty training. Pups are similar to humans, what goes in must come out. The schedule for the pup's nutrition format will determine the pup's toileting schedule.

Experts recommend feeding or watering a pup on a preset schedule. Potty time should follow the pups' nutritional format by approximately twenty minutes. The pup's digestive system requires time to process the nutrition before preparing it as waste products. The pup or dog should be granted potty time but be cautious of the pup using the allotted time as play time, rather than pottying. Carefully monitor the pup's actions, remain consistent, and repeat behavioral patterning for better consistency.

The age of the pup or dog will preset the expectancy of toilet necessity. For example, pups should be capable of holding their waste for one hour per month of age. A four-month-old golden should be capable of holding their waste for four hours. Do not wait for the last minute to take the pup potty, but this does grant a time frame for the owner's convenience. Scheduling provides a less complex format for the animal to obey.

Maintaining toileting consistency continues with the location for potty training. A pup being outdoor trained should be leash led to a designated site for potty time. This consistency will teach the dog the difference between play time and potty time. The pup will familiarize itself with its potty versus play locations.

Indoor training requires designating a specified location as well. Owners must indicate the exact area, pad, and/or litter established for toileting. Once this place has been determined, experts recommend maintaining its location as to not confuse the pup. Confusion may lead to indoor accidents. Implementing the three basic recommendations; consistency, repetition, and patience will get owners through this difficult stage of life.

Potty training time should be segregated from other training periods. The pup will learn to complete its potty business at a quicker rate and have an easier time learning potty rules if they are not blended with other activities. For example, enforce the potty area and schedule, and then return the pup to the house door. If the owner wishes to enjoy play time or additional training work, start fresh. For example, allow the pup to finish its business, walk to the chosen house door, and have the pup sit as to recognize the doorway. The owner may then call the pup out to a new area of the yard for a game of fetch or to practice obedience commands. Potty training outdoors may often be mixed up with additional training needs, separating them maintains pup consistency and reduces confusion.

Indoor training locations must remain consistent as well. Owners should designate a specific area for indoor toileting. The litter box, toileting pad, or whichever means of toileting is preferred should be preset and remain in the same location. Pups will become confused if this site is altered; thus resulting in accidents. The toileting site must be maintained for cleanliness. Experts recommend locating this site in an area without heavy traffic, as to allow animal privacy and comfort. Do not place this site within the dog's immediate crate. Crate extensions or directed regions of extended crates may be used for absent periods.

Rules of potty training shall become normal activities as pups/dogs learn the skills required to maintain their potty health. Pottying is after all, an act of nature. Owners may become more lax with requirements; for example, combining potty and play time, once the rules have been mastered. Owners requiring stricter behavior may choose to continue the regulations preset at the beginning. The owner's preferences will govern the lifestyle shared by pet and owner.

Please allow us to exemplify our personal preferences regarding potty training methods. Being parents to a large family, human and dog kids, we have established a mutual agreement, "Let Them Be Little", a song which prompts parents to appreciate the growing stages of a child's life. This song, by singer Billy Dean, has taught us to respect a child or in special cases, pups age-appropriate capabilities. Keeping this in mind and heart has granted us the gift of patience, a significant training tool for all kids.

The format, "all for one and one for all" is a game plan we highly recommend. It may be very helpful for any family or couple to predetermine a puppy training contract before purchasing a pup. This contract may be prepared with mutual respect for one another, as well as the pup. The suggested materials within the contract may include command language, training methods, schedule breakdowns, activity charts, nutritional arrangements, medical agreements, and future responsibilities. This contract will permit the relationship between people and pet to advance in a healthier manner.

Potty training requires consistency, repetition and patience; whether an owner is a professional or private individual, these three components play key roles in getting the job done. Being very familiar with the potty training concept, "diaper duty", puppy training was dealt with as we had managed previous potty duty.

Step one, selecting our choice of training methods; our personal selection being outdoor training. We prefer outdoor training because it works well with our lifestyle. We dislike the interior maintenance of pads and soiled papers. Our large yard welcomed the fertilized soil from potty markers; wow, our grass was a brilliant green.

Selecting the method led us to step two, determining our pup's schedule. My wife and I base our pup's schedule according to our work schedule. We take our pups out for potty when we awake early in the morning. My wife works at home, hello, she is an author, and I work in a factory. We set the pup's potty breaks based on the early morning starting point. Potty breaks are preset by the age; for example, two month old goldens must break every two hours, whereas, five month olds break at the five hour marker. Once the first break has been fulfilled, we begin breakfast. My role is to prepare dog food, while my wife prepares our family's breakfast. My wife monitors the pup's break times based on the pup's nutrition schedule and break time markers. She works through the day with these factors in mind. My training role begins when I return from work. My first job is to check on the pup's daily activities. Once I am aware of the schedule, I react to what is next. I am sure to work in sync with my wife. We made an agreement to train as a team or partners. This means, that we use the same commands, rules, and formats to assure consistency and reduce complexity.

Training commands should be short, firm, and consistent. Pups will remember, relate, and respect commands they adapt to with rapid reaction. Altering commands or the language of the commands may result in pup confusion. A preset puppy contract may list command terminology for all family members to implement in training; thus reducing chaos amongst family members.

The most famous command "potty outside" rings through our house of dogs. Using short commands calls the dog's attention in a simplified form. Drawing attention to preapproved terminology helps us to remain on a consistent track; therefore, our pups learn at a healthier rate.

Mutual training methods also call for designating commander behaviors such as, always using a leash to walk the pup to the potty area, training the pup to heel on an individual's left side, and ending potty time by returning the pup to the home before starting another activity.

Additional training tips may include showing the pup the found accident; showing the pup the accident makes it alert to it realizing that you are aware of what it did; therefore, it didn't get away with anything. Once the pup has been shown the accident, state, "potty outside", or select your terminology of preference. Take the pup outside on its leash to its preset area for potty time; the pup may not go again, but it will realize where it should have gone. Praise the pup for going out, regardless if it did or did not go; it will grow to realize that it is a positive thing to go outside for its potty time.

Owners should remain strict, but gentle. Pups require a positive tone of voice to learn skills. The harshness in an owner's voice may scare the pup; therefore, blocking the training attempts. Learn with the pup; it will be a wonderful experience for both man and beast.

Obedience training is the root to all training. It is best to begin obedience training as a pup; however, dogs are capable of learning obedience at all stages of life. Please locate a training facility or course close to your home. Leash training must be taught before teaching additional commands. The list of obedience commands for level one include but may not be limited to: sit, stay, come, and heel. Obedience level two commands may be stated as, but are not limited to: sit, long stay, settle, down, heel, and road safety. Advanced commands also labeled as dog tricks may be stated as: sit pretty, fetch, rollover, and hide and go seek. Basic or level one obedience training must be mastered before leading into advanced or trick training.

The first rule of obedience training is to have fun working with your dog; "all work and no play" makes for a bad experience.

Level one obedience training requires repetition, consistency and patience. Please remember pups and dogs, not to mention some owners/handlers have a short attention span; we highly recommend keeping training sessions short and fun for best results.

Leash training is the first basic obedience command we will discuss. Leash training begins with collar training. Please allow us to suggest the training method we have found most successful. Pups may be introduced to collars at five weeks and older. We usually begin using collars during the sixth week. My husband and I use the collars as markers; an indication of who has selected which pup. Place the collar on the pup for twenty minutes at a time. Repeat this act three times per day. Continue this process for one week. Increase this time by an additional twenty minutes, four times a day, for an additional week. The pup should be adapted to wearing its collar full time within two weeks. Do not over tighten the new collar. The owner should be capable of sliding one finger between the pup's neck and the collar. Check the sizing of the collar as the pup grows. Massage the pup's neck and collar to make the pup feel more comfortable. Talk in a cheerful voice as the collar is placed and checked. These actions will make the collar a positive issue.

Leash training will follow once the pup has become comfortable with its collar. The next step is to clip a short leash to the collar. Allow the pup or dog to wander freely; do not implement restraint. The pup will play with the leash. This grants the pup or dog time to accept its presence. Stop the pup from chewing on the leash by passing it a treat. The pup will learn that the treat is better than the leash. Remove the leash when the dog or pup tire of it or do not show any attention towards the leash. The pup or dog has just learned; leashes aren't so bad.

Owners should remain consistent with leash introduction. The next step is to place the leash on the dog or pup and call the dog or pup to your side. The pup may require a few calls. The use of treats may help alert the pup or prompts the pup or dog to come to you. Once the pup or dog has arrived, grant it one treat, pick up the leash end and hold it for a few minutes. Do not force the pup or dog to stay, allow the pup or dog to walk away with the leash. This maneuver shows the pup that the leash is not a threat, but there is more to it than it being a toy. The pup and owner will both note progress.

Please place the dog's leash on its collar and prepare for lesson four. Do not apply force, allow the leash to enjoy ample slack. The pup or dog will naturally follow its owner as the owner maneuvers around the home. Place the leash handle in your hand. If the pup pulls, stop walking immediately. Call the dog or pup back to your side and then begin walking. Praise the pup for returning to your side; this will teach the dog or pup to want to remain by its owner's side. The dog may stop and sit down when practicing leash work. Stop; do not jerk the dog to stand. Talk to the pup and praise it for trying. The pup will become excited and will stand to walk. Begin walking once the pup or dog is prepared. These actions will work with the animal's natural instincts; therefore, learning is fun.

Step five is to begin showing the dog or pup that the leash is a tool not a toy. Training a dog not to pull its leash is not difficult. Owners or handlers must enforce their role as the leader. The owner should alter the direction of the walk. Do not allow the dog to become too familiar with the walk pattern. Owners should change their walking direction every time the dog or pup pulls on its leash. A second method of stopping the dog from pulling is to stop the walk, call the dog to the owner's side, enforce the sit position and begin the walk once again. Praise the dog for returning to the owner's side and for sitting. Praising the dog will encourage further listening skills. Repeating these actions will exhibit consistency. Remember, repetition, consistency and patience will produce successful leash training.

Owners experiencing difficult times with leash training may require the guidance of a professional trainer or tools. Professional trainers provide additional training methods involving the implementation of advanced collars: chokers, electronic, and spiked. Trainers may recommend heavier, stronger, or more restrictive leashes to discipline the dog while leash training. Please seek the advice of a professional for appropriate use of advanced training equipment.

Sit is the most valuable of all level one or basic obedience commands. There are several suggestions regarding the instruction of the sit command. Please consider our recommendation. We believe linking hand signaling and verbal verification together to be a strong method of teaching the sit command. Please begin with placing the dog on its leash; this provides the dog with a secure restraint as well as a solid measure of attention. The owner or handler should alter the leash from the left hand to the right, as to free the left hand. The left hand will need to be freed so that it can maneuver the appropriate hand signal. The firm, yet cheerful vocal command, "sit", should be spoken as the motion is being conducted, use the left hand to point downwards, showing the dog the act of sitting, place the left hand on the dog's rear quarter, firmly, but not cruelly push the dog's rear quarters downward while using the right hand and leash to raise the dog's head to a height appropriate level. Please repeat this lesson until the dog has learned the skill.

Success will be achieved once the dog has learned to sit upon command. Implementing the use of the leash is step one of this process. Once the dog has learned to sit upon command using the leash, remove the leash. The owner or handler should implement the verbal sit command and hand motion of pointing downward, without the leash in effect. If the dog will not perform the sit command reimplement the leash. The sit command will require a great deal of repetition. Remain consist in practicing this act. Do not get upset if the dog needs a great deal of practice to learn the skill. Practice this skill throughout the dog's day. For example, stop a few times while on a walk just to instruct the dog to sit as a practice measure. The owner may be watching the dog at play and request the dog to sit as a reminder of the command. Remember, practice makes perfect.

Stay is the second basic command taught to dogs. We suggest using the verbal signal and hand motion in unified sync. The stay command will follow the sit skill. Teaching this task may involve the use of the leash. Please follow these steps: step one: instruct the dog to sit, step two stand in front or along the side of your dog, step three: state, "stay", step four (do this step in sync with step three), place your hand, palm towards the dog, in front of the dog to show him the signal to stay and step five: slowly walk away repeating stay and signaling stay. Dogs will move towards their owners, when this occurs, it will require the owner or handler to firmly, not cruelly motion the dog back to the original sit position, repeat the signal and command for stay and once again attempt walking away while the dog maintains its placement. The owner or handler should be capable of walking away at more and more range as the dog learns the skill. The dog will require less repetition as the skill becomes mastered. This skill serves as a wonderful security for preventing accidental issues and difficult situations.

The come command is our third basic obedience skill. There are many methods of teaching a dog to come. This command demands an immediate reaction; when an owner commands "come", it means "now". This response may be taught with three signals: vocal, hand and whistle. The whistle exhibits two short blasts of the whistle to signal the dog to come. The hand signal involves the view of the stay signal being brought upwards and then dropped straight down towards the ground. The verbal command method is the most common form of signaling come. Hand signaling is convenient when noise may bother others in the area and it is a productive means of getting the dog into the habit of checking in on its owner. Whistles are useful when the dog cannot hear the owner due to excessive noise, distance or voices. The come command may work as such: state, "dog's name, COME", using a cheerful voice hand signal or both together, if needed, clap your hands, this will get the dog to move, usually towards the sound or signal, it may be appropriate to have a reward awaiting the dog, this will encourage the dog to actually come. The dog will learn to come quickly in hopes of receiving its treat. Treats are not always a piece of food; the reward may be a nice pet or ear scratch. Dogs react to this command because they enjoy being close to their owner or friend.

Stop is a strong command which is usually implemented for safety. This command may save a dog's life in cases of stopping the dog from traveling on a road or into traffic. This term is also applied in the hunting arena. There are several methods of teaching the stop command. One method is to use a rope technique. Place the dog on a rope. The dog may begin in the sit and stay position. Call the dog, "come", granting the dog room on the rope to move. State, "stop", freeze the rope, forcing the dog to stop because it hasn't rope to move. The dog will learn to stop as commanded because it will dislike the jerk or force of the rope. A second method may be dogs previously skilled to sit upon hand signal and come on instant command, will learn stop very quickly. Place the dog in the sit stay position, walk a large distance from the dog, command come, run quickly away from the dog, allow the dog to pick up a good pace, then alter your direction towards the dog, shout stop as you signal the stay signal enforce this act with true gusto. The dog will react to the powerful action. The dog may think the owner is a bit foolish, but the actions will definitely be memorable; thus, the command is deemed a success.

Heel is a vital command. This command is one of safety and convenience. The dog should walk in sync with its owner or handler. Implementing the leash as a guide tool makes this command work more smoothly. Once the dog has learned the skill, the owner may choose to walk without the leash. Teaching this command may involve placing the dog on a leash, stand alongside the dog, and begin walking with the dog. Draw the leash to a tight grip as to prohibit the dog from drifting too far away from your side. The hand signal for this command is a slap on the owner's leg. The dog will hear the command, "heel" and note the hand signal, "slap" then realize it should be walking along side its owner or handler. The dog should begin stepping once the owner has begun his or her first step. The dog should not take lead nor walk in front of its owner. The owner should draw the dog back if it becomes out of form or control. Slapping the leg reminds the dog of its natural place alongside of its owner. This command may be conducted without a leash, once the dog has mastered the skill and may be granted more freedom.

Down is a command instructing the dog to remain down; it should not jump up on a person or specific place or item. Please attempt this maneuver: apply the knee against the dogs chest, this is the hand, knee signal, state "down", and instruct the dog to sit. Once the dog has respected the sit command, owners may choose to reward the dog with a treat or loving pet. Repeat this action until the dog learns it will be treated with love and respect, when it treats others with love and respect. The dog will halt jumping up and begin approaching people and things in a calmer fashion. This skill will be a welcomed success.

This book will not discuss advanced skills or commands. Level two and above commands will cover a great deal of tasks. Please seek more specified materials or research trainers of such skills. Future materials may briefly touch upon advanced skills. Please consult arena training for more details.

Personal Reflection

"All work and no play"

Our son, Michael Logan Bauer, was born with an illness entitled double malasia. His medical journey began with his birth and continues yet today the struggle was real! This gorgeous little boy was forced to endure numerous respiratory hardships. He spent a great deal of his infant and toddler days at children's hospital in Milwaukee WI, where several specialists dedicated a great deal of effort towards his survival.

Developing a progressive treatment program was the task at hand. Michael's pediatrician was brilliant, diagnosing him accurately as well as promptly. His diagnosis was challenged by many physicians from the moment he arrived at children's hospital. Months of: repetitive testing, medication alterations, experimental procedures, and diagnosis changes created a great deal of hardship for not only our son, but every family member. We learned, definitely the hard way, that the medical staff could not conquer all of Michael's medical needs on their own. Michael endured many long time stays at the hospital always anxiously yet fearfully awaiting his dismissal to go home. We wanted him home, but were scared to death that his respiratory would fail which could lead to many critical medical hardships. Michael had gone code blue seven times within the first three months of his life. One specific scary memory is that of our trip to the circus; luckily all of our family members had received training in infant cpr because Michael had gone code blue in his car seat on our way to the circus. Maranda watching over her brother closely began hysterically shouting "Mikey's blue! Blue like a Smurf! He's not breathing help him help him" she quickly got him out of his car seat, calmly started breathing into his mouth, passed him to me in the front seat where I continued cpr as Bruce rushed directly to children's hospital. Physicians said Michael was ok this time. The time had come to think out of the box, that's right we had to recognize there was a vital link missing along his medical chain of team members.

His team was blessed with numerous medical specialists, who provided outstanding care along his medical journey. Family members stepped up loving him with every heartbeat and helping in any way each and all could. Advanced medical equipment provided incredible control over his harsh situation. This young man required twenty-four hour a day seven day a week quality care; one lost minute could've cost him his life. The answer was obvious, the missing link, was our son required a respiratory service dog.

Our son now a toddler continued his medical journey, winning a few battles yet facing the raging war. Michael was definitely a challenging child, always ready to push his medical team to their breaking point while wearing the most adorable smile on his face. He was truly a demanding, mischievous, intelligent, loving, challenging, unique child. Being that we were very experienced and knowledgeable in the service dog arena we knew that good would not be good enough, the dog our son needed had to be above and beyond a miracle dog. We couldn't trust an outside resource, our hearts led us within our own golden retriever family. Our beautiful Anastacia birthed a brilliant female pup we named Avanue Grace aka Michael's Ava baby. This pup exhibited exceptional skill. Bruce began her training regimen at seven weeks of age. She excelled in all of her day-to-day obedience 1-2-3 training programs. Ava and Michael bonded beautifully. Training specialists stepped in to assist Bruce; thus, providing Ava and Michael with a respiratory and behavioral training regimen which was sure to lead both of them down a successful pathway.

Ava was an incredible blessing. Her respiratory skills included but were not limited to: alert, massage, focus fetch, and cpr technique. Her behavioral skills included but were not limited to: companionship, tricks, block, cover, search, and yet many more. Michael and Ava were quite the team always have one another's backs. Our family could relax because we trusted her skills; she was definitely a vital member of his medical team.

All work and no play doesn't keep the dr away. Michael's medical team, including Ava, was sure to stay tight on his heels monitoring every breath he took. Ava performed her job role with intense skill and true hearted dedication. Everyone on the team respected every team member.

Michael was challenging everyone, demanding he wanted to be a normal kid. His respiratory system had progressed, therefore allowing physicians to reduce, but not stop Michael's medical monitoring. There was finally room to breathe. Let the fresh air flow as they say. Michael was so excited and wanted to take advantage of every healthy minute, it was the first day of summer the sun was shining brightly, and our family pool was open for business.

Michael was all smiles and smirks walking out wearing his new swimming trunks. Bruce checked the water temperature, lighting system, and ladder security before allowing the kids to jump into the pool. Michael went in and out of the pool a few times allowing himself some breathing breaks and rubbing Ava's belly. Bruce called "Last chance to swim" so our smiley young son hurried over to the ladder for one more swim. The girls were sunbathing, Brian was playing with Ava's momma Ana, when Bruce and I heard Michael yell "Help!", Bruce quickly jumped into the water, but was pushed aside by Ava. Ava Grace quickly got Michael safely to the water's side securing his safety. Bruce realized Michael had a very suspicious smirk on his face as he carried Michael out of the pool to lay him on the blanket on the grass. Ava stood at full alert watching every move her youthful recipient made. All was quickly realized he pulled a prank on his pooch; the question was who was the better prank puller, Ava vs Michael.

Ava quickly licked his neck and rubbed her cold nose all over his belly tickling him to the point of no return. He rolled around and rolled around trying to get away from his very irritated service dog. She knew he had pulled a fast one and she wasn't going to let him get away with it. She started licking the bottom of his feet until he tried to get up and run away. Guess who's get away wasn't so smooth, Michael Logan Bauer lost his swimming trunks. The wet trunks dropped to his ankles; his little feet kept moving while his naked little heinie ran across the yard. Ava Grace following quickly behind tightly gripped my son's swimming trunks in her mouth. Bruce shouted "Michael, Ava has your swimming trunks!" after repeating this a few times, Michael finally turned around, he reached down to grab his trunks, but failed. Ava turned around and ran the other way, the chase was on, Ava held onto those swimming trunks with dear life just out of reach. The backyard was filled with laughter. Bruce finally commanded her to give back the trunks "Game over" lesson learned.

Michael and Ava's adventures continued through time. Afterall all work and no play isn't the healthiest way to honor life; life is to be lived with true respect and gusto. Sadly, our beautiful Ava Grace has passed to heaven, but it is thanks to her hard work, loving dedication and invaluable skills that our son Michael Logan Bauer continues to walk this Earth breathing, growing, living his life with respect and appreciation. Ava truly earned her mark of gold.

Chapter 9

Career Arenas

The life of a golden retriever may take many turns. Golden retrievers are capable of fulfilling numerous arenas because of their unique character traits: intelligence, appearance, ambition, energy, and disposition. The combination of these features has developed a dog of master skill and heart.

Career roles for goldens include, but are not limited to: service, therapy, police, military, show, commercial, hunt, pet, search and rescue. There are many factors used to determine which role or roles are best suited for the specific golden in question. Please note the following descriptive paragraphs for role identification.

Role identification may be judged by a collaboration of the pup's owner, handler, trainer, veterinarian, and professional in the career field. The first traits to be evaluated include: maturity, endurance, and energy. Dogs will undergo a two part physical. Part one is a complete health checkup: hip certification, eye certification, heart certification, inoculation record, club registration, (confirming breed standards), endurance screening and behavioral patterning. The second part of the examination is based on emotional standards: temperament evaluation, behavioral patterning, and skill testing. The results of these exams will assist in role determination. Apprenticeship in temporary role placement is a key tool in finalizing arena assignment. Goldens may attempt placement in more than one role before permanent fields are stabilized. Many goldens work in one arena and later transfer into a second as they age. This exemplifies the skill versatility of goldens.

Service arenas warmly welcome the golden retriever. The service industry employs goldens for numerous types of medical challenges: blind, seizure, diabetic, hearing, behaviorally challenged, physically restricted, and yet many more regions. Servicing is a one on one role; service dog verses service recipient. Institutions work with highly skilled trainers and medical experts to determine, not only if servicing is the correct placement, but which service industry is the dog most suited. Testing is based on the following factors: dog's physical report, human's physical status, dog's temperament study, and the human's psychological foundation. For example, a highly energetic dog may be too much for an older recipient to work with; whereas a more relaxed dog may be a healthier match. The programs conduct multiple testing formats to assure a loving and lucrative match is found.

Blind guide servicing is the most popular working arena within the service industry. Leader Dog and Seeing Eye Dog are two top ranked schools providing the blind community with trained service dogs. Guiding dogs are trained to protect their masters from environmental obstacles, dangerous situations, and provide a sense of freedom. Blind people have great respect for their working companion. These miracle workers assist in numerous daily functions that sighted people take for granted. A guider may assist a blind person in traveling throughout society. There are numerous obstacles: stairs, traffic, curbs, trees, and other people, which a trained guide dog assists a blind person to cope with as they maneuver through society.

The absence of a guide dog may result in several harsh scenarios: the blind person may be forced to restrict their travel, the blind person could face harm, and the blind person may have to absorb the fees of a human employee for care. These harsh realities are the very reason behind the promotion and training of goldens within the industry.

All good things have a negative side. Guide dogs cannot read nor drive a vehicle, advancements yet to come; however, the skills the dogs do portray are highly respected and graciously appreciated. Guide dogs are truly a blind individual's best friend.

Service dogs for the blind must graduate from basic obedience classes with flying colors. Once the field trainer is assured of the dog's accomplishment, the dog begins two forms of training: socialization and environmental. These forms of training develop the dog's ability to work in the community or surroundings in which it will be located. For example, blind service dogs must learn to be comfortable with all forms of transportation. Blind people are known for traveling via city bus, local taxi, passenger train, and various airplanes. The dog quickly learns to perform their skills in all transportation situations. Environmental training involves socializing the dog throughout society. Dogs must become comfortable working in public: stores, restaurants, libraries, hospitals, banks…etc. Trainers show the dog how to maneuver throughout a variety of situations. Traffic is a major lesson in itself. Dogs are shown how to react to the traffic. Blind people are kept safe by their watchful companions. Obstacle training requires a great deal of repetition and consistency. The dog learns what to watch for and how to maneuver around the obstacles. Trainers manipulate preset signals and verbal commands to educate these faithful workers. Blind students are taught to use the predetermined terminology and signals to reduce complexity and benefit from the dog's training status. Please contact training facilities for more detailed training information.

Medical experts applaud the aid provided by seizure dogs. Specialists have noted numerous seizure related illnesses: epilepsy, allergy, and mental health, just to mention a few, may greatly benefit from the care of seizure dogs. The service dog is trained to alert the individual to an oncoming seizure. This alert may grant the person time to react, preventing or limiting the level of harm faced by this person. The dog may be trained to urge a secondary person for assistance in cases of their companion being beyond notification or self-assistance. For example, an individual coping with an epileptic seizure may require the dog monitoring the person's safety; the dog may remove obstacles such as a sharp object or certain material the person may strike; thus keeping additional harm from the person. A person involved in an allergic seizure may be prenotified as to an odor; the dog may smell this odor before the person would notice it. The dog would guide the person away from the odor's location; thus preventing the seizure from occurring. A third scenario may involve the service dog requesting aid from a second party; trained servicers are taught to search for a professional such as an officer and draw them to the sight in need; in times of severity, the dog may simply approach a stranger and attempt to draw the person to the sight at hand for aid.

The most common form of aid assistance provided by a service dog in this industry is onset alert. The dog senses the onset of a seizure; using the alert method, the dog notifies the person that a seizure is coming. The person can take self protective measures to prevent or protect themselves from the seizure.

The quantity of seizure related injuries has greatly decreased thanks to service dogs. This industry has noted tremendous advancements throughout recent years. The United States has welcomed numerous research teams from: England, Canada and Germany in hopes of developing techniques for seizure treatment and detection. The service dog training programs have carried incredible influence with the studies currently being conducted by these expert professionals.

Goldens instinctively recognize the chemical reaction related to their companion before the onset of a seizure. This step, recognizing a seizure at its onset, need not be taught, it is natural. Step two, alerting the companion requires training the dog as to what method it should use to alert its companion. This skill may be taught by playing a game entitled, "alert". This game teaches the dog to alert their companion using a specific alert method that has been pretrained. One type of alerting is having the dog paw at the companion's leg to receive a reward. A second alert method may be having the dog bark to alert their companion. One may ask, just how does that help an individual who has seizures? The dog learns that it receives a reward when it is seizure time. Trainers teach the dog to paw at the companion's leg to receive a reward. The game is to be played only at seizure time; this highlights the dog's reaction to a seizure. Please note this scenario: the dog will recognize the chemical onset of the seizure, it is anxious because this means it is game time. The dog paws at the companion's side, playing the game, and gets a reward for alerting the companion. Dogs do not get to play or receive a reward for pawing when a seizure is not coming. Dogs learn this game or task very quickly. Dogs portraying anxious, nervous and or deep caring personalities are well suited for this service industry.

The American Diabetic Foundation has dedicated recent funding to the training of service dogs for the purpose of assisting serious diabetic youth and adults. Research has proven that trained expert dogs; especially goldens, can recognize the onset of diabetic complications. Medical professionals have reported that well trained dogs may be capable of signaling the onset of diabetic seizures and shock. The service dog can alert the ill individual of an oncoming problem so that the person may react while still capable of requesting aid or preventing or limiting oncoming harm. Service dogs in this industry are currently being advanced with rapidly growing educational markers every day.

Trainers have chosen to implement the "alert" game for this medical challenge. The dog will note the chemical change that occurs in the diabetic's body. The dog is taught that when it notices a chemical change it should notify, by implementing the recipient's chosen method of alert. The dog will be rewarded for alerting the person of the problem. This game saves lives. The individual may have time to react to the problem in two ways: seeking medical aid and self-treatment. Additional training methods have been attempted; however, the alert method has gained rapid and prominent success.

Hearing impaired people share great respect for service dogs. Service dogs are trained to notify the hearing-impaired individual to many environmental issues: sounds (alarms, phones, announcements . . . etc.), traffic, emergencies, and yet much more. Service dogs protect their hearing-impaired companion from any source of harm they may encounter in society. They provide a healthy sense of freedom from obstacles; many take for granted what the hearing impaired hear loud and clear, silence. For example, a public fire alarm, a nuisance, that is unless it is a real emergency; a hearing-impaired person may not realize to react within a timely fashion; therefore, is subject to harm. The service dog would quickly alert the individual to react and guide the companion to safety. A second example may be something as simple as a hearing-impaired person setting an alarm for work. It could ring for an hour and yet it wouldn't wake the hearing-impaired person; the dog would awaken and alert the companion to wake. The service dog wouldn't bark to alert the hearing-impaired person, it may nudge the individual or tap the person with a paw. Signaling methods are specifically trained means of assisting the companion. Trainers select professional methods with proven success for service work.

One of the largest specialty fields in service training is entitled Behavioral service. This arena includes but is not limited to: PTSD, Autism, Down syndrome, COVID syndrome, Depression/anxiety, and additional mental health disorders. This arena is massive due to the extensive variety of behavioral challenges within our society.

Physically restricted individuals share enormous appreciation for their working companions. Disabilities such as limb restrictions, back disorders, limited maneuvering and yet additional issues welcome the aid of a skillfully trained service companion. A service dog may assist a disabled individual to move into or out of bed. The skilled dog could help with chores; servicers can place laundry into the washing machine, remove it from the washing machine and place it into the dryer, remove it from the dryer and place it in a basket; oops, can the dog fold laundry, another advancement yet to come, so life's not perfect! Service dogs can help with dishes; parents have trouble getting kids to do the dishes. A service dog will clear the dirty dishes after a delicious dinner; no, not by licking the plates clean, but by placing them into a sink or designated place. The dog may remove items to be placed in the refrigerator, cupboard, or specified region. The disabled person enjoys a game of professional fetch; pets may enjoy a simple game of fetch, where as a professional servicer plays for work. The service dog is trained to fetch or retrieve items it is instructed to get for the disabled individual. These dogs may retrieve a long list of necessities: medications, shoes, clothes, remotes, keys, and of course many more selections. These companions are the disabled person's right or left hand/foot best friend.

Please note the specific skills these service dogs are trained to perform:

1. Retrieving: dogs are taught to retrieve hard to reach or manage items upon demand. Service dogs have the intellect to retrieve items by specific name.

2. Finding the phone: mobility service dogs are trained to locate the phone by scent and bring it to their companion.

3. Pulling a wheelchair: Mobility service dogs are trained to pull a wheel chair with the use of a harness or strap.

4. Hold it: This term or skill refers to the dog holding an item for the companion. The dog will pick up and hold an item for the companion.

5. Get help: Mobility service dogs are trained to get help for their companion. These dogs make others alert to the needs of their companion in times of danger or trouble.

6. Opening doors: These dogs work with attached ropes. Homes are prepared with ropes placed on doors, cabinets, and specified items.

7. Push buttons: Mobility dogs are trained to push specified buttons on command. This is a great help in elevators.

8. Getting dressed: This service dog is trained to help remove socks and shoes, as well as additional clothing items. Luckily, these dogs do not mind stinky feet.

9. Lights: Mobility dogs are trained to turn lights on or off based on request.

Mobility service dogs work very hard to make life less work for a physically challenged individual. "All work and no play" is for the dog, not the companion . Skills specifically designated in the arena of mobility may include, but are not limited to: assisting the recipient with dressing/undressing, shifting a recipient from one position to another, transporting a recipient from one location to another, bracing a recipient for additional support, fetching a recipient's required objects and yet of course many additional skills. Honestly, this work is completed with tremendous skill and heart; therefore, it truly is a labor of love, one smart game.

Therapy is a wonderful arena for golden retrievers. This field of work may be the golden's primary or secondary placement. Goldens may be employed in an arena such as: service, commercial, police, or search and rescue throughout their young adulthood and later transfer into therapy as a means of working retirement. Pet golden retrievers are the most popular for being implemented as therapy workers. Therapy dogs provide loving companionship to those in need of emotional support. Candidates for therapy assistance may include, but are not limited to: terminally ill, mentally challenged, long term illness, restricted seniors, challenged youth, and educational facilities.

The role of a therapy dog is that of love. These precious goldens enjoy sharing their life with those in need. Qualifications in the therapy arena include: obedience, socialization and behavioral, training. Professionals also conduct temperament evaluation, physical screening, and community acceptance testing. Therapy dogs may be noted recipients of the Canine Good Citizen award.

Volunteers may attend training programs educating them on the roles of therapy dogs. The human is trained as well as the therapy dog. Volunteers, owners, handlers, and candidates may request therapy dogs trained for additional skills such as tricks, but this is not the typical performance or requirement. A well behaved loving dog is a welcome visiting companion. Sometimes a person just needs a best friend.

Police are proud to introduce the canine training programs as being one of the most remarkable throughout the working dog market. Human officers are paired with their working dog, as would two humans be paired in the field. The police dog carries rank, as does a human officer. Rank is based on the dogs' educational accomplishments and field achievements. Training programs designate watch, guard, and detector tracking and public awareness as being the specified roles within the police arena.

The role of watch dog is one of security management. Watch dogs are trained to watch over the material, person or location. Training teaches them to signal, usually by barking, if a disturbance or potential issue occurs. Role identification prohibits the watch dog from further action.

Guard dogs are trained to protect, to various levels: watch, attack, and/or seize, the designated item, individual, and or location. These roles are clearly marked for appropriate dog assignment. For example, goldens being of a gentler temperament, are usually placed in the role of watch, rather than guard, or may be assigned as guard position one, rather than a sharper or more aggressive position. Police trainers investigate the breed's status, standards, and skills before role establishment.

Police agencies employ numerous detector dogs. These dogs are trained to sniff out potential harms: bombs, drugs, bodies, agricultural products, odors, and additional situations or scenarios. For example, a cadaver dog is a detector dog specifically trained to detect dead bodies. This type of police dog or military dog may locate the bodies of victims; families of the deceased individuals may be dearly saddened, but appreciate the closure related to finding their loved one's body. "The nose knows" is a well suited cliché for this role. Locations for this employee may include, but are not limited to: schools, postal industry, airports, hospitals, shipyards, and hotels. This arena may be traced back to the original role of the golden, the hunter.

Tracking dogs are implemented in searching squads. These highly intelligent dogs exhibit high levels of energy and endurance when searching for criminals, bodies, materials, and additional scenarios. Tracking dogs have genetic connections reflecting upon inherent qualities of hunts from long ago.

Public awareness is a vital position for a police dog. These dogs are used to circulate public awareness messages, encourage educational programs, and promote environmental safety. Public awareness dogs may be professional commercial dogs; however their training must include police as well as commercial training. A police dog's role is to protect society above all costs.

Training regiments are strict. Police dogs must execute: sit, stay, down, and heel. Dogs must remain on the handler's side or within a distance of fifty feet. Accuracy is required; dogs are allotted one fault within five commands. The commands may be verbal or signal. Stay and heel are rated critical. Sit and down are rated as semi critical. Patrol dogs must perform all movements in sync with their human partner. This style of maneuvering is taught to a team, MWD, manned with dog, for the provision of police security.

The MWD team must prove their capabilities in the following tasks: forward march, rear march, column left, column right, and halt. Recall is vital, handlers must be able to recall the dog at a distance of fifty feet and stop the dog at a distance of twenty five feet using the sit and stay commands. The dog must then react to heel via vocal command. Recall is ranked semi critical.

Patrol dogs are required to master the police obedience course while off leash. Dogs must complete this task at a marching pace. The dog must maintain attention to all commands, not simply run the course as it chooses. Dogs are allotted two errors per command.

Patrol dogs must master six phases of aggression management:

1. False run: The dog must remain in the sit stay position and not move when a person approaches. This is ranked as critical.

2. False run into a bite: The dog must remain in a in the heel, sit, or stay position until commanded to attack at the verbal command, "get them". The dog must hold the bite for ten to fifteen seconds. The dog must release on the command, "out". The dog must release on the second command, only one infraction is allowed. The dog must return to heel upon command. This is ranked critical.

3. Search and attack: The dog must remain in the heel, down, or sit position when commanded tostay. The dog must hold its required placement while the partner searches a decoy while off leash. The search consists of patting down all limbs and the torso of the decoy. The dog must attack the decoy without command if the decoy tries to attack or flee the handler. This attack must complete the attack by full mouth biting and holding the decoy until the command, out is sounded. This is ranked critical. One verbal correction is allowed. The dog must return to heel upon completion of attack. The dog must not attack the decoy unless under command.

4. Search and call: the dog must hold the stay command until released. The dog must maintain the heel, stay, or down position. The handler searches all limbs and torso of a decoy. The handler moves to a position about two feet to the right and ten feet to the rear of the decoy placing the decoy between the dog and handler. The handler commands the dog to heel on leash this is ranked critical.

5. Standoff: The dog must remain in the stay position until commanded to "get them". One infraction is allowed. The dog will chase the decoy until noting the command, "out". The MWD will return to the heel placement. This is ranked as critical.

6. Escort: The MWD must heel upon command escorting the decoy for at least twenty yards. The MWD is on leash. Attack is not allowed. This is ranked as critical.

Out and Guard

1. Field interview: The dog must remain in the heel, sit or down position when commanded to stay. The MWD must not attack when a person approaches the team. This is ranked critical.

2. Field interview into an attack. The MWD must only attack upon the command, "get them". This is ranked as critical. The dog must bite with a full mouth bite and hold it for ten to fifteen seconds. The command, "out", must be respected by the sound of the second command. One infraction is allowed. The dog must return to the guard position once the bite is released.

3. Search: The dog must remain in the sit or down position as commanded. The handler repositions the decoy about ten feet from the MWD. The search will consist of the limbs and torso. The handler places himself behind the decoy and instructs the dog to heel. This is ranked critical.

4. Standoff: The MWD remains on leash unless released. The dog attacks only upon command, "get them", and must stop attack upon command, "out". The MWD must then sit, down, or stay upon command. One infraction is allowed. The dog must react by the second command. This is ranked critical.

5. Escort: The MWD must escort the decoy for at least twenty yards without biting the decoy. This is ranked semi critical.

6. Building search: The MWD will search and locate a decoy inside of any building and show it to the handler. This may be completed on or off leash. The handler must recognize a response, false response is not permitted. This is ranked critical.

7. Gun fire: The dog must remain calm and under control. The dog must attack only if under command. This is ranked as critical.

8. Scouting or patrolling: The dog must be capable of locating people by scent, sound, or sight. Decoys hiding one hundred yards upwind should be detectable. Decoys hiding two hundred yards are not detectable. This is ranked critical.

Narcotics Detection Dog Certification Standards

MWD is required to carry a 90% success rate of detection with no more than a 10% fail rate.

1. The locations for certification evaluation must vary for accuracy. Sights such as: clubs, hotels, automobiles, offices, banks, etc... provide excellent variations for training.

2. Training aids must remain hidden from the MWD team. The aids used must be allowed out for a maximum of thirty minutes.

3. Training aids should be hidden from floor level to a maximum height of ten feet. This is to monitor air currents. The handler must be capable of detecting the dog's behavioral changes.

States may enforce different laws and punishments regarding drug crimes. Please note state guides for more detailed training issues. Regulations for MWD teams may differ based on the specific laws.

Explosion Detection Dog Certification

Explosion detection dogs must qualify with a 95% with no more than a 10% false report.

1. The locations for testing must vary: office buildings, automobiles, hotels, apartment buildings, banks, clubs, schools, etc... to provide realistic sights.

2. Explosion training aids must remain hidden and may not be put in place more than thirty minutes before evaluation is conducted. Training aids should vary in size, location, depth and amounts. These variations will stand as realistic testing scenarios.

3. Explosives must be hidden from floor level to a maximum of ten feet so that a dog and handler can distinguish air currents and detect behavioral changes.

The MWD explosive team must adapt the training keys: repetition, patients and consistency to produce successfully trained dogs. The teams work continually to increase the capabilities of the dogs and handlers.

Specialized Search Dog Team Certification

1. The list of obedience commands exemplifies the degree of communication skills within their relationship.

2. The dog must respect all obedience commands: sit, stay, down, heel, and come not only at its handler's side, but as far away as fifty feet as well. One infraction is allowed. The commands heel and stay are ranked as critical. Sit and down are ranked as semi critical.

3. The search dog must follow all maneuvers in sink. The dog must be capable of heeling while executing all commands off leash. The commands include: forward march, rear march, column left and column right and halt. These are rated as semi critical.

4. Recall will consist of calling the dog from a distance of fifty feet and stopping the dog at a distance of twenty five feet. The dog must respect the sit or down command. The dog will then be called to the heel command. This is ranked semi critical.

5. The dog must complete the obedience course at a marching pace off leash while at heel placement with its handler. This course will be spontaneous and free from predetermination. There may be but two corrections.

There are numerous arenas within police dog training. States vary in the requirements and regulations for dog training. Please research multiple programs and police agencies for further details regarding the roles of police dogs and the dog training industry.

Military life empowers the skills of working dogs. Master trainers educate military personnel as well as the working dog itself, as to the invaluable role of the dog's position. Dogs in the military receive training similar, yet more advanced, to that of the police dog. The tasks required for a military dog mimic those expected of police dogs. Watch dogs may monitor enemy locations. Guard dogs may be used to stop a criminal act against our country. Detector dogs could prevent a bomb from causing great damage. Tracking dogs could search for hidden materials. Public awareness dogs could spread the message of safety throughout a foreign land. These dogs may only differ in the types of locations they work, the level of endurance required per job and/or the term of performance. Many military retirees are reassigned as police dogs. The military dog may continue the avenue of role reassignment and train as a therapy or pet dog once completing its term of service as a military and police dog. This dog works hard to be "man's best friend".

Show dogs are incredibly gorgeous masters of beauty and skill. This popular arena may be divided in three rings: obedience, conformation, and agility. Please detail the role designation of these rings.

Obedience is defined as a set of rules or regulations a dog must master to accomplish good behavior. Pups begin obedience training early in life. Puppy classes will teach pups to: sit, stay, come, stop, heel, down, and so forth. Variations in class material may be based on instructors' preferences. Advanced obedience courses may portray methods of skill building, seeking to teach tricks such as: fetch, hide and seek, water retrieval, search, and yet many more. Obedience shows concentration on the mastering of basic skills. Once the dog has conquered the tasks of obedience, the dog will implement these talents in all show rings.

Conformation is the second ring within this arena. The American Kennel Club and the Golden Retriever Club of America have set predefined standards which must be honored by all goldens. Golden retrievers have historically placed very well within the conformation rings. Current breed standards may be sighted by referring to the American Kennel Club regulation listings: coloring must be within the ranges of goldens: light, moderate, and dark; white, black, deep red and shades of reddish tones are not permitted. Judges will determine if a dog is allowed to compete. The size of the golden must be qualified to be permitted in the show ring. Please see the A.K.C. postings for size regulations. Dogs must be six months of age to compete. Shows are designed with levels based on dog's age status. Judges will check for coloring, size, and behavior, accuracy in show style, presentation and breed traits. Goldens have a very successful history in this ring.

Agility is the third ring within this arena. Many participants note it as the most enjoyable of the rings. Audiences enjoy watching the dog and handler perform many skills as they enchant the ring. The obstacle course is one of the favorite skills performed. This task exhibits team work through a timed obstacle course of tunnels, jumps weaves, and poles. Please note American Kennel Club regulations for more details.

The most popular and successful training technique implemented in all show rings is entitled, shaping. The method involves building a specific behavior by using a series of small steps to achieve the necessary behavior. Shaping is based on the dog's natural learning abilities. Trainers implement a distinct signal or marker to highlight the correct behavior. The dog receives a reward when it hears the signal. The dog will be pleased to hear the signal which marks a correct behavior; it is well aware that it will be rewarded when it hears the signal. This system is noted as "clickers". Clickers are the most common signal, but trainers or handlers may select their own signal method.

Please note these scenarios: Joy needed to improve her golden retriever's behavior in the conformation ring. Tripper, a one year old golden was having trouble with the judge checking his bite. Tripper would back up or run off every time the judge would approach his mouth. Joy implemented the use of a clicker to shape Tripper's behavior. Joy would sound the clicker then praise Tripper. He quickly learned that the clicker sound meant he would get some petting and love. Joy would touch his nose and mouth, sound the clicker and pet him for a few minutes. He would not hear the clicker nor get loving attention if he was not well behaved when she touched his nose and mouth. She added a twist to the game. Joy asked her friend, Cori to assist in teaching Tripper to allow his mouth checkup. She would begin by clicking if Tripper allowed Cori to touch his nose and mouth. The click meant a lot of love. Tripper did not hear the click if he wasn't good; therefore, no love or petting. He quickly learned that the good behavior, clicker and praise were related. He now allows anyone to check his bite.

The second scenario involved Marci and her golden two year old Lucy. Marci adopted Lucy from a local shelter. Lucy had been abused; therefore, she portrayed a fear of being touched by strangers. Marci knew this was unhealthy. The clicker method would work well for altering this behavior. Marci simply began by sitting near Lucy, sounding the clicker and giving her a treat. This step was repeated four times a day for four days. She advanced this to extending her hand to Lucy, softly petting her back, sounding the clicker, and then rewarding Lucy. She repeated this four times a day for four days. Marci altered her simple touch to massaging Lucy all over, sounding the clicker and rewarding her dog. Lucy quickly related touch, click, and reward. Marci requested her friend, Joe step into the process. He attempted to sit near Lucy. She was a bit spooked. He picked up the clicker and softly spoke to her. She remained near him, but she carefully watched him. He would talk a moment, click and reward. She liked this game. He moved closer to her, clicked and rewarded. Joe actually touched her side, clicked and rewarded. Step by step click to treat, they grew to be friends. Shaping worked very well to earn both a successful relationship.

Many trainers enjoy using the clicker method for training dogs to perform in agility contests. Allow us to play out a training session for training the dog to maneuver through a tunnel. The dog is introduced to the tunnel. Step one, show the dog the tunnel, sound the click, grant a treat. The dog will learn to like the sight of the tunnel. Step two, prompt the dog to step inside of the tunnel, sound the clicker, and grant a treat and boom, the dog likes being inside of the tunnel. The trainer moves to step three, maneuvering through the tunnel. Many trainers prompt the dog to follow the trainer through the tunnel. The trainer will usually click the signal as they are moving, granting treats as they move. The dog learns that moving through the tunnel earns a treat. Step four, the trainer will exit the tunnel at the end, click the signal, grant a treat, tunnel work is accomplished. The final step is to maneuver this in a flowing motion. The trainer approaches the tunnel, click, enters the tunnel, click, passes through the tunnel, click, exits the tunnel, click then grants a treat. The dog will learn to maneuver hearing the clicks to earn the treat. Repetition, consistency and patience will gradually teach the dog to quickly start, maneuver, and exit without hearing clicks until achieving the tunnel. The quicker the dog moves, the quicker it gets a treat.

Trainers do use other training methods; however, clicker methods or signal methods have earned great success. Trainers prefer to remain secretive; sharing their training tips and formats requires enrollment in their courses.

Commercial dogs "strut their stuff" as well as do show dogs. These professional actors and actresses adore the attention of the public's eye. Trainers educate dogs in many skill levels. The dogs are noted for their: appearance, skill, talent, temperament, and personality. Commercial dogs must adjust to the world of performance: direction, cameras, lights, audiences, and roles. These dogs working roles entail a network of complexity the commercial dog must master if they are to reach "top dog".

Trainers teach levels one through four obedience to all dogs employed in the commercial industry. Level one obedience: sit, stay, come, down, and heel is the building blocks for all additional commands. Level two commands: stop, fetch, roll over, lie down, and seek are used in a number of programs, shows and movies. Trainers are known for using the clicker tool to shape the behavioral skills required in this level. Levels three and four involve stunt work. Trainers may implement the shaping method, but they may back it up with multiple reward methods as well.

Hunting dogs fulfill a glorious historical reflection. The golden being a master sporting dog has graced the hunting field with superior skill, ambitious energy, and powerful endurance. A golden's ability to track, flush, and retrieve their game proves their abilities in this arena. Hunt and field tests are promoted by the American Kennel Club on a regular schedule. The sporting industry offers additional testing markets; please note hunting clubs for multiple resources.

Hunting dogs may be trained as pointers, dogs which indicate the location of the pray by pointing their nose and tale to the designated direction. Goldens are more typically known as flushers; they locate the scent and flush or move the bird out of hiding for the hunter to spot. The next step is to implement their skill of name sake, retrieving; once the bird has been shot, the golden will track the fallen pray and bring it to the hunter's side. Hunters have applauded goldens as superior hunting tools, "a hunters best friend".

Hunt training begins with designating the game of choice. The next decision involves determining the choice of weapon: gun, archery, trap, and so forth. The third factor calls attention to the terrain identification; the terrain may alter how the dog performs. The forth component is climate. Hunters must monitor the climate conditions; extreme heat and cold are very hard on a dog's health

Once these factors have been dealt with, the actual training methods may be implemented.

Hunting Recommendations

1. Carefully select the correct breed of dog. Golden retrievers rank on the top of the sporting dog list of favorites.

2. Pups are usually better to begin hunt training while older dogs require more time and acquire less skill. Pups should be seven to ten weeks.

3. Train the dog to hunt using scent, rather than vision.

4. Nutrition is vital. Provide appropriate nutrition; monitor weight and quality. Exercise dogs throughout the year; do not allow the dog to pass on exercise during off season. A complete health regiment is crucial to the hunt training.

5. Prepare the dog for its climate.

6. Be sure to hydrate your dog. Hunters require a healthy provision of water.

7. Confirm all obedience commands. Praise the dog for its obedience skills. The dog will appreciate the praise and feel encouraged to continue a learning pattern.

8. Teach the dog to respect the hunter. Hunters should also respect the dog.

9. Purchase a new electric collar. This tool will assist in correcting problems. This is an optional choice.

10. 1Train the dog to recognize scents; bird wings are highly recommended. Remember the hunter owns the wing; the dog may not chew or destroy it. The wing is to provide a sense of scent to attract the dog to the bird's territory or location.

Hunting Tools

1. Purchase a hunting collar; an electric collar is recommended, but is not required.

2. Purchase a whistle for signaling the dog. Distance plays a key factor in the dog's ability to follow a command; the loud whistle is easily heard. Therefore, the dog can respect the command by whistle.

3. Purchase a check cord for training the dog to line and return.

4. Hunters should purchase a blank pistol. This will associate the sound and dog without fear factors coming between the dog, hunter, and game.

5. The use of scented decoys or bumpers work wonders. The bird wings are fabulous.

Hunting is a serious issue that is best taught as a very fun game. Dogs learn better when they are having a good time. Fetch is a dog's favorite activity. Hunting dogs truly enjoy fetching scented decoys or bumpers. This game must begin with the dog having previous knowledge of all level one obedience commands. Trainers will assert two additional commands: fetch and back. The trainer will post the decoys in sight; these are titled marks. Decoys that are placed in hiding are titled blinds. The dog will be instructed to fetch the mark, "Anna fetch"; she will retrieve the scented decoy and bring it to her hunt trainer. Trainers may choose to hold the dog back for a bit, teaching patience and respect. The dog will learn to watch the game, not rush it until the hunter is prepared. The hunt trainer will release and command the dog to retrieve the mark. Use the obedience command stay until the dog is released to retrieve. Blind fetch means that the dog needs a service dog to help find the game; just kidding. It refers to the scented bumpers being hidden. The dog will be released with the command back. Trainers will command, back, sending the dog to search for the scented decoys. The dog will locate the decoys or bumpers and retrieve them for the trainer. Dogs instinctively scent; therefore this game is a blast for the dog.

Trainers enjoy teaching dogs to point. Hunters like to instruct the dog to hunt in the designated direction. Achieving this may be done using the method entitled lining or hunting in line. Trainers line up a series of scented bumpers or decoys. Send the dog to fetch the decoy. The dog will naturally retrieve the first one in the line. Praise the dog's action and send him down the line, decoy to decoy, praising each one retrieved. This will teach the dog to follow the direction of the line. The dog learns patterning or line retrieving quickly.

Hunters work the dog to retrieve the bird the hunter designates, not the bird the dog prefers. The dog may note two birds down. One may be dead; therefore, it can wait a minute. The second may be injured and fluttering; therefore, must be retrieved immediately. How does the hunter train the dog to retrieve the designated bird, rather than the one it chooses?

The task of designating the game may be taught by implementing the tool known as the check cord. The check cord will restrain and focus the dog. Toss a mark in a specific direction which is noted by the dog. Point your hand or arm towards the mark. Release the dog stating, over, to retrieve the mark. Remain patient, consistent and repeat this game numerous times. Praise the dog for its hard work, "all work and no play makes the game work not fun, so who wants to play it, no one".

This game may be advanced by adding more decoys to be retrieved. The hunt trainer should place the decoys, point to the one chosen for retrieval and release the dog by command to retrieve the designated decoy. The game will require a lot of repetition to be mastered.

Level three of this game involves using a mix of marks and blinds. The dog may become confused when the hunter points to an area where the dog cannot see a decoy. The hunter must continue pointing and sending the dog to the area. The curious dog will rush to take a look; the scent will lead it to the blind. Patience, repetition, and consistency will work to master this skill. Praise the dog with rewards to encourage the dog. Have fun learning with the dog.

Quartering is a term referring to the dog scanning the field or territory being hunted. The dog should always be located in front of the hunter. This is different than the training fields: behavioral, socialization, and obedience as previously discussed. Dogs should be located in front so that they can flush the bird or locate the bird on point for the hunter's convenience. The dog is trained to maneuver the field in a zig zag pattern, scanning or quartering the field for game. This action will alert the dog to scents or sights. The dog will react to its findings by flushing or pointing its found game. If nothing is found, new ground may be covered.

Pups or dogs must be taught to remain in front. Trainers may teach a pup to do this by maintaining appropriate distance and reversing placement. Pups like to walk very close to a hunter's heels. The hunter can position the pup by picking up their foot and lightly kicking the pup. The pup will dislike the kick, remember not harshly, and move away from the hunter. The pup may overreact to harsh kicks by moving too far away and feeling abused or grow fearful. Be careful with the level of force used to teach the pup placement. The second training method is simple. The hunter needs to move the dog to his front, but the dog or pup is walking behind, simply turn around, placing the dog in front. The hunter should turn directions every time the pup or dog are located behind the hunter; thus, placing the dog in front of the hunter. The dog will quickly learn its appropriate placement. Once the dog has learned its place, it will begin maneuvering the territory and quartering for game.

Force fetching may be a difficult task to teach. Progressive training courses teach us that goldens do not refuse to fetch because of resistance or refusal, but that the dog simply is having an issue understanding the command. Force fetching is the act of commanding the dog to grasp and retrieve the designated item regardless of the dog's reasoning for not retrieving, dropping its hold or retrieving an incorrect mark.

The goal of force fetching is to train the golden retriever to fetch, grasping the object or game using appropriate force, as not to harm the object or game, hold it without dropping it premature to its destination, bring it to the hunter's side and release it upon command. This goal may be achieved through a technique known as pressure training.

Pressure training involves using pressure levels to enforce the dog's actions. The dog should not be harmed. The appropriate level of pressure should be safely determined. The dog will learn that it can control the level of pressure applied by performing the correct actions.

Pressure Methods

1. Ear pinching
2. Toe hitch
3. Electronic collar

We must strongly state, that hunters must apply pressure with great caution. Dogs must not be abused. Dogs may have a difficult time realizing that their actions will regulate the pressure. Hunters should consistently show the dog the object or game of retrieval to encourage the dog to pick it up; therefore, stopping the pressure. Rewards such as treats may assist in force fetching. Praise or treats may be granted once both components have been met; the moment the dog accepts the object being fetched, stop the pressure and then grant praise, a nice pet or pat works very nicely.

Gun hunting is the most popular style of hunting. Dogs enjoy gun hunting when trained correctly.

Noise association is the beginning to training a dog to accept the sound of a gun. Pups should be gradually introduced to loud sounds. Playing music at reasonable levels is a great start; gradually increase the volume, but do not blast it. Bang kettles together; some say this sound simulates gun fire. Fireworks usually create a strong fear amongst dogs; attempts at associating fireworks and gun fire have proven unsuccessful. Firing a blank gun off in the distance is very affective. The use of rewards is helpful. Sound the blank gun and pass the dog a treat. Bang the pots and grant the dog a treat. The dog will associate the loud sounds to a treat; therefore, it will like the loud sounds because it associates it to a treat. The dog will soon realize that loud sounds are simply part of their life.

The sight of the gun will quickly excite the dog. Hunting dogs associate the gun to going hunting. Hunting is a game involving exercise, fresh air, scents, game and playing with their best friend.

Gun shy dogs are easily managed. The loud sound cannot be withdrawn; gun hunters need their guns; therefore, associating the gun to joyous activities will calm the shy dogs. Please follow the scenarios below.

1. Jon was having trouble with his golden retriever cowering every time the gun was fired. He had it; so he took his dog to a nearby kennel. The trainers knew exactly how to deal with the problem. They placed the dog inside of a kennel to associate with the other dogs. He did well; enjoying the other dogs. The trainer walked outside and fired a blank gun. The dog rushed into the interior kennel. The trainer waited for lunch time and prepared his routine. He walked kennel to kennel and filled their dishes. He walked outside and fired his gun. The shy dog rushed into the interior kennel. The trainer closed the door; therefore, the dog didn't eat. He repeated this activity three times. The hungry dog learned that all the other dogs kept eating while he was so hungry. He flinched, but remained by his bowl. The fourth day was the best; he didn't even flinch. The dog was calm and happy to enjoy his meal.

The dog was then tested in the field. He was so excited with the birds and scents that the gun fire didn't spook him. The dog is now a master hunter.

2. A second scenario is about a golden retriever male named, Smacks. He was one year of age. Smacks was so scared of gun fire that he would bark every time he heard gun fire. His owner had decided to sell him.

Smacks was a gorgeous golden with a loving heart. His owner's wife was in love with him, so he was not being sold. She brought him to the trainer in hopes of helping her husband and dog.

The trainer began with playing music at various levels in the kennels. He added banging a few pots at lunch time and exercise time. Day by day he introduced not only loud sounds, but granted a treat each time he made a loud sound. The dog was quick to associate the loud noise to the treat. Smacks grew to listen for the sound and look for his treat.

The trainer tested him in the field. Smacks heard the gun fire, didn't jump, and looked in the trainer's hand for his treat. The trainer switched to a wing, rather than a treat. The dog liked the scent and was very happy. Smacks is happy, the husband is happier and the wife is the happiest.

There are several methods of training dogs to work with guns. The mutual goal is to get the dog comfortable and excited with the gun and gun sound. Please contact local sporting clubs for additional training methods. Veterinarians may offer additional suggestions as well.

Golden retrievers love water. Training goldens to water hunt is a dream job. Pups are easily trained to master water training. Dogs may require more time and input, but they catch on to the fun quite readily.

Splish splash, the lake is better than a bath. Slow and steady are the keys to introducing pups and dogs to water. New experiences require patience. The first visit to the lake, river, pond, or stream should not involve tossing the pup into the water to see if it can swim. Owners should check the water temperature before entering the pup into the water. Water should be a minimum of 62° F for a pup or dog. Cold water is harsh for the pup or dog to handle; training the animal is more difficult in colder water because the animal concentrates on the discomfort instead of the techniques. The optimal temperature for training falls between 70° F and 85° F. The second point to monitor is the water activity. Pups and dogs learn better in calmer water. Rivers with rushing currents or lakes with big waves draw the animal's attention towards the activity and away from training techniques. Moderation is the third step to introducing pups and dogs to water. Walk in the water with the pup or dog. Make it fun and interesting. Play with the pup by splashing it a little. Show the dog how nice it is to cool off in the fresh water. Do not enter too far unless the pup or dog show the interest naturally. Bring a water toy for the pup to play with in the water. Toss it a few feet away. Fetch is a natural instinct. The distance should increase with every visit to the water. Be consistent; visit the water three to five times a week for a few months. The pup or dog will become comfortable and grow excited about their fun water visits.

The pup or dog will learn to connect the water game with land retrieving by playing games. Trainers recommend a game of fetch that links both terrains. Begin by introducing the dog to the water. Walk around in the water a few minutes. Toss a water toy into the water near the pup. Command it to pick up the toy, "fetch". Repeat this game a few times until the dog is comfortable with its response. Advance the game by tossing the toy farther. Begin tossing the toy towards the shore line. The dog should learn to retrieve the toy on either terrain and bring it to its owner's side. Toss the toy in both directions, water and land, to teach the dog to fetch it and return from and to its correct destination. This game will grow more exciting as the distance increases. Implement patience, repetition, and consistency to make this task enjoyable to master.

Trainers recommend transferring from a water toy to a bird decoy once the dog or pup has become acclimated to the water. The reason for this is to maintain familiarity in the hunting arena. The dog will better relate to the decoy bird; do not think that the toy represents a game and the decoy indicates serious work, this is all a big game to the dog. The point is keeping the game fun and exciting; the more the dog enjoys playing, the better it gets at playing, the better the dog hunts.

Training tricks are numerous. Please enjoy this scenario. Jason had accomplished teaching Crews, his six month golden sire, to swim and retrieve in shallow water. Issues arose when he began tossing the decoy into the lake at a distance of thirty feet or more. The dog would start swimming towards the decoy, but lose track of it while swimming. The trick to this is to throw small pebbles in the direction of the decoy. The dog will notice the toss and action and head towards the drop. It will eventually learn to maintain its attention and keep its game or toy in sight or scent.

A second scenario is the problem facing Don and his bitch, Candy, a two year old golden. Don had purchased her from a rescue. She had been abused by a previous owner. Don and Candy spent four months socializing. Their relationship was very strong. He was ready and raring to move it to the next step, water.

Don began by walking the shore line with her twice a week. He advanced to tossing her favorite toy into the water a couple of feet. She was just fine with getting her paws wet, but disliked it when the water level reached her belly. Don attempted to draw her into the water by showing her how much fun he was having in the water. She watched from the beach. Don brought treats, but wasn't sure how to use them towards training. Luck struck, a professional trainer was fishing one day and stepped in with a bit of advice.

He recommended using shaping methods to work her towards deeper water and then cross over to fetch and retrieving. Don had used shaping for socialization, so he was aware of how to implement the technique. He would walk her near the water, click and treat. He graduated to tossing her toy in the water, have her grasp it and return to him, click and treat. Candy began moving deeper and deeper, click and treat. She knew the routine. This worked.

Don followed the trainer's suggestion; he began using the bird decoys. She was hesitant at first, but she liked the bird scent. The scent became her treat. Candy was water retrieving within a month.

Wonderful, the dog is working great in the water. The time has come to introduce the gun along with the water. There are numerous methods available in this field. We will discuss the techniques we have found successful. We urge all interested parties to research hunting clubs, professional trainers, and additional resources for more information on training techniques. Please enjoy our outlook along the pathway to learning about water hunting with a golden retriever.

We cannot stress enough how important it is to remember the keys to all training: patience, repetition, consistency, and fun. These basic points will guide owners and dogs through all training methods. Water hunting follows the same guideline. Steps one: familiarizing the gun and dog and step two: water comfortability must be drawn together for water hunting success. This goal may be easily achieved. Trainers recommend beginning by firing a blank pistol off as the hunter tosses a decoy into the air. The dog will associate the shot to the falling decoy; thus simulating the act of shooting a real bird. This technique is easily transferred to actual hunting as the dog prefers the real scent of the bird to the decoy scent. The dog will travel through the water maneuvering upon command to retrieve the shot game. One, two, three; hunting success.

Goldens are master hunters on land and water. Training methods, hunting tools, and a healthy relationship between the hunter and dog are the key factors for developing a healthy and happy hunting experience.

Search and rescue is an arena critical to society. These working dogs save lives. Trainers of various arenas partner to train a collection of skills required by the search and rescue dogs. Goldens were welcomed for their magnificent intelligence, incredible endurance, terrific detection, remarkable tracking, outstanding energy and loving hearts. Roles of this arena include, but are not limited to: tracking, herding, rescuing, and retrieving materials, individuals, and locations.

Professionals turn to the expert skills of search and rescue goldens during times of tragedies. For example, search and rescue dogs saved many lives at the site of 911 in New York. Search and rescue goldens were employed in the massive search conducted in the Rocky Mountains of Colorado; a seven hour search resulting in the rescue of two young climbers. One may review public, police, and military records to note numerous reports of successful search and rescue stories. The combination of all of these features has earned the golden retriever, "the mark of gold", within the search and rescue arena.

This career arena prefers to begin training pups as of twelve weeks of age; however, older dogs showing potential are welcome. The first step in training is general obedience. Pups and dogs must master obedience before entering the search and rescue programs.

Wilderness search and rescue, one specific branch of search and rescue require certification in the following: tracking, trailing, air scent, and cadaver. Trainers insist on training dogs in tracking and trailing, then air scent. It is strongly noted that dogs trained for air scent have an extremely difficult time learning air scent and then track or trail. Professionals believe that air scent is very easy for dogs to learn; therefore, the dog feels it doesn't need to display the skill or energy to learn tracking and trailing. Dogs mastering tracking and trailing naturally pick up air scent very rapidly. Goldens have been called the power house breed of wilderness search due to their prominent skills in all of these search branches.

Alert is the technique of notifying that the dog has located an object, body or location. The act of searching is very instinctive for the search and rescue golden; it is actually more work training the dog to alert an official as to its findings. Goldens have tremendous scent capabilities. This natural born talent is united with expert training techniques to master a lifesaving skill.

Dogs work wonders when searching for people or cadavers. The human body releases scent from 40,000 skin cells per minute; each individual releasing cells unique to each body. The dog's nose can track these odors for great distances and lengthy times with ease.

Tracking dogs are trained with a 20 to 30 ft. lead and harness. The dog wears this harness when training; the dog relates the harness to tracking; therefore, it focuses much better. Tracking is trained with many techniques. One of the basic methods is to have a familiar person drop a scented article near the start point, create a scent pad, then walk 10 to 20 ft. while forming a treat pathway along the distance. The person then hides in an easily detected location. The handler shows the scent pad to the search dog and commands, "find" or "search". The dog searches out the person and receives great praise and treats for its success. These exercises will be conducted on numerous terrains. The distance increases as the dog becomes more affiliated with searching. The handler will use less treats as the dog becomes more experienced. The short searches begin in a straight line. The exercises may appear simple, but they teach the beginning skills that lead to master search and rescue teams.

Phase two is more intense. The distance is greatly increased. Locations become more complicated: heavier vegetation, larger buildings, and mixed terrains. The dog will continue using the scent pad and treats, but increase distance and time. Once this phase is conquered, the dog moves on to faze three.

The third phase uses the scent article, but it doesn't use the scent pad. The level of treats is greatly reduced. The tracking involves curves, closed trails and other more difficult terrains. Trainers are clocking for an accomplished time of ten minutes or less to find the person. This work requires repetition, patience, and consistency.

Phase four involves much more detail, variation and complexity. Two subjects are used to train the dog; one is the victim and the other is the distraction. The two people will be passed the scent article. They walk or move for a controlled distance together, then separate. The dog must track the one holding the scent article. The dog and handler should be capable of tracking trails that are up to 24 hours old and a distance of 1 to 2 miles in distance. The dog and handler should be capable of maneuvering all terrains. Dogs working at this level should be prepared to take the tracking dog test.

Trailing dogs work similarly to the tracking dogs. A scent article so that it can locate the scent of the subject being trailed. The dog will begin on harness and lengthy lead. The trailing dog may cut corners by using scent identification to locate the subject. The dog will learn by following scents and treats. The progression is identical to the patterns of the tracking dog.

The air scent search dog works off lead scanning an area for a human scent. Handlers allow the dog to drift as it searches; exhibiting well-earned trust between handler and dog. The dog must sound "alert" when it locates the subject. The dog may bark to alert the handler.

Dogs must be trained to bark upon command. Bark command is difficult for the dog. Trainers begin training this command as young as possible. This command is usually taught using treats and praise.

Team searches begin with runaway searches. The dog is held by a familiar person. The handler excites the dog. The handler runs off into the wind and hides. The dog is in full view of these actions. The handler is holding the dog's toy. The familiar person releases the dog, commanding, "Find" or "search". Great praise and treats are the dog's rewards for finding its handler.

Searches are kept in a straight line and must be into the direction of the wind. Trainers increase distance and time to increase the dog's capabilities. The terrain becomes more difficult to challenge the dogs. Step by step life savers are being developed.

The dog is required to bark as an alert in this phase. The dog is commanded to "speak". The dog is actually commanded by the subject, definitely not what will occur in reality, but it is effective in training. Once the dog has sounded the "alert", the handler moves in to aid the dog. The dog will be rewarded.

The process involving a refined is different. Once the dog reaches the subject, the handler calls the dog to return to the handler. The dog is then commanded, "Refined". The dog will then respond by refined the subject or answer to the command, "show me". Training sessions remain short, lined and cheerful. Terrain is altered to present challenges. Climate variations are also implemented to develop a stronger sense of realism. Rewards are used to encourage interest and success.

Dogs conquering previous stages are prepared for blind searches. This refers to dogs seeking unfamiliar hidden subjects. The dogs work upwind. Terrain is altered for complexity. Training sessions remain short. Rewards are used as an encouragement. Repetition is required to teach this skill level.

Phase work continues with the addition of more difficult terrains, longer distances, increased times and more subjects. The searches are no longer straight lines; thus the dogs have their work cut out for them.

Search and rescue dogs must master the three components to be certified for search and rescue. Training must be a fun skill building adventure shared by handlers and dogs. Someone's life is depending on the success of a search and rescue dog team.

Pet goldens may have the hardest, yet best, job of all. The complexity of family life is quite a challenge. Goldens are loyal and loving. These wonderful pets dearly respect their owners. Owners must maintain obedience standards; the owner is the master, the golden is the pet. Many working dogs retire from their careers to be welcomed into the homes of loving pet owners. Goldens are praised for their hearts of gold; "a golden is man's best friend, as is a man golden's best friend".

The field of working dogs continues growing throughout society. Medical experts implement these highly trained dogs as a medical aid or tool of talent in more and more positions at a rapidly increasing rate. Professional experts promote educational efforts and skill advancements in police and military field studies. The progress levels improve with leaps and bounds as funding, education, training and implementation become more secure.

Career markets for master dog trainers, educational experts and medical specialists have opened their very welcoming opportunistic doors. Volunteers are urged to participate in training and medical programs. Society as a whole is prompted to research educational materials and apprentice structured positions within the numerous regions of working dogs. No human can take the dog's job, but society can certainly establish powerful measures for developing highly skilled programs for multiple advancements. Future accomplishments may be based on the success and promotion of yesterday's achievements; growing through the years thanks to "man's best friend".

Personal Reflection

"Opposites Attract"

"No way, not those two, ya got to be kidding! ", laughed all of our friends. Bruce and I were complete opposites. He was the hunter and I was the business lady. We sure shocked everyone when we not only started dating, but announced our engagement six weeks later. Talk about people whispering at the wedding; we think most of our guests showed up just to be sure it was true.

Are you familiar with the old cliché, "like mother, like daughter"? The theme traveled through time with our golden daughter, Miss Abby. Abby lives to go hunting. She struts her stuff through the woods, proving her master hunting skills on every excursion. There's no stopping this hot little lady.

Abby was interested in one big hunt, a man hunt! It was love at first sight. Introducing Abby's first love, Big Ben, a service guide dog. He thought she was a hotty. She worked her stuff; the cute little tail wag, turning her head, rolling her eyes, sniffing his cute butt, oh yeah, one huge case of "puppy love".

Big Ben's owner, Scott, my computer teacher got a kick out of our dogs falling head over tails in love. Our friends cracked up, "no way, those two, you got to be kidding". I think I remembered hearing those words once before. The hunter verses the guider, total opposites, totally in love.

Our personal intention was to purchase Abby as a show dog. She was beautiful, graceful, and obedient; mastering all the marks of a champion show girl. Parents can dream, but kids make life a nightmare. It wasn't really that bad. I'd spend hours bathing, grooming, and prompting her for a show; she'd spend ten minutes chasing a bunny through the muddy woods. Parents' rules blown away, dog rules take control. What a life!

My husband was in hunter heaven; he was smirking with all his glory. My precious show girl turned master hunter. I think the two of them preplanned this journey.

Scott, a wonderful friend and brilliant teacher introduced Big Ben into our home as his service guide. I was in need of new computer equipment and training because of a fire we had endured a couple of years ago. Scott instructs computer technology within the homes of visually challenged individuals. I was so excited, I'd been waiting for months to get my new equipment and meet this miracle teacher. Bruce and I walked out to greet them; Big Ben was proud at work, guiding his beloved master to our front door. We weren't the only curious parties; Abby was checking him, Ben, out.

Big Ben was such a gentleman. He was hard at work guiding Scott, and sneaking peeks at Abby. He demonstrated his servicing skills and flirting talents like a true professional. This young man was definitely husband material.

Do you have any idea how difficult it is to concentrate on computers when there are two dogs playing the dating game right at your feet? Ben struggled to hold his place by Scott's side. Abby was sure to maneuver around the room; therefore, drawing as much attention as she could. Ben truly earned his salary; employed as a highly skilled guider and engaged as a terribly talented boyfriend. Abby, strutting her womanly powers, oh yeah, the hunt was on!

These two golden retrievers are lovable opposites. Ben works hard to guide Scott around the world. They have enjoyed being traveling partners for many years. Scott depends on Ben's master service training as they tour business and personal sights on a very hectic basis. Abby's drive for hunting is energized by her intense passion and instinctive scent in the field. This is like comparing "Lady and the Tramp".

Do you hear wedding bells? Goldens have excellent hearing. Kids, they just jump into relationships without thinking things through. Parents must step in and sort out the details. Ben would have made a wonderful doggy son in law, but two big issues were brought to light. The first subject was in regards to having a family. Abby is a gorgeous bitch for superior breeding; poor Ben is a neutered, but handsome young man destined to serve his master alone. The second obstacle dealt with was residential status. Ben's family enjoyed city life. Abby couldn't go hunting at the mall; bunnies and birds aren't allowed. The two love birds would have to settle for being pen pals. Guess whose owners had to do the writing for them!

Chapter 10

Rescue Shelters

Golden retrievers require and deserve a great deal of love, attention and care. Please do not purchase or adopt a golden retriever until all care provision subjects have been appropriately addressed. The physical and emotional damage caused by inappropriate purchasing or adoption are quite severe.

Dogs may be relocated in shelters or rescues because of cases involving neglect and abuse. Leading causes of neglect and abuse include: puppy mills, negative breeding, housing complications, family difficulties, dog behavioral issues, and financial problems. Hardship circumstances such as: accidental injury, owner related health matters, financial burdens and personal tragedies play an unexpected role in this spectrum as well. Regardless of the cause society must react by establishing care provision facilities, which can appropriately provide: care, training, and affection for these worthy animals. There are numerous hardships which must be considered within the complexity of this subject: finances, legalities, locations, and training, just to list the tip of the iceberg.

America's leading cause is inappropriate puppy purchasing. "It's puppy love", or is it? Individuals purchasing a pup must prepare a life plan for their puppy. Prove you love the pup by carefully detailing a plan for the pup's needs.

PUPPY LIFEPLAN

1. Puppies are cute and adorable, but remember they grow up.

2. Research dog breeds before purchasing a pup of an unfamiliar or later disliked breed.

3. Investigate the breeder. Do not purchase from puppy mills. Conduct interviews with the breeder and confirm breeding information.

4. Review personal finances to establish a plan for all expenses: training, medical, nutrition, housing, and supplies.

5. Confirm housing and yard provisions. Be positive the home is secure; monitor land lord situations, city ordinances and residential regulations.

6. Prepare for training expenses and schedules.

7. Price all required supplies for availability and financial commitments.

8. Confirm scheduling, pups and dogs require love and attention.

9. Discuss the purchase or adoption with all individuals concerned.

10. Take time to be sure of your decision.

Puppies deserve love and respect. It is not healthy to purchase a pup knowing the above steps have not been positively confirmed. Owners must be sure of the seriousness involved with pup purchasing and adoption.

Negative breeding creates a serious issue for rescues and shelters. Negative breeding may refer to breeders who conduct or allow breeding of inappropriate bloodlines. Blood lines showing indications of health issues: aggression, in breeding, hip dysplasia, heart troubles, and other genetic problems should not be continued. Medical experts recommend reproduction control for all dogs indicating negative health issues.

Puppy mills are largely responsible for inappropriate breeding issues. These hardships may be noted as: over population, weak blood lines, false breeding, illegal marketing, illegal registration, illegal licensing, and inappropriate care provision.

Over population is a serious issue. Puppy mills will over breed bitches and sires to produce pups for markets. Over breeding creates numerous health issues such as bitches premature death, damaged hips, weak bladders, strained reproductive systems, and yet many more health conditions have been reported. Research has shown that many of the pups born of over breeding are infected with numerous health conditions. Puppy mills have been noted for cross breeding; yet claiming pure blood lines and falsifying paperwork. Breeders have also been noted for breeding bitches and sires past their appropriate age bracket; bitches and sires should usually halt breeding at about eight years of age. Pups born of parents past appropriate ages may be struck with serious health risks; the most common being the mother passing away in delivery. Please seek educational information from additional medical experts regarding hardships connected to puppy mills.

Housing is a subject related to the complications of golden retriever neglect and abuse. One issue regarding housing is that of new owners not preparing for their new pup purchase. Many owners are rental candidates. Land lords can set regulations prohibiting dogs. Many renters believe once their land lord sees just how adorable their pup is all will be ok; unfortunately, that is not the typical story. Renters have gone to extremes to hide new pups; pups get bigger, noisier and more active, not as easily hidden. Dogs outgrow apartments; lack of yards, restricted areas and small living space create problems. The pup may have been approved by the previous land lord; however, a sold building, may inherit a land lord who is not as welcoming of dogs.

Property owners are not free and clear of housing hardship issues. Neighbors may create static. Dogs developing behavioral issues can cause complications. Barking, straying, and aggression present problems. Training may solve the problem, but owners must be willing to seek and implement corrective aids.

Owners should research city ordinances or county regulations before purchasing a dog. Limitations are predetermined and are publicly noted for society's inspection. Please reference laws for pup or dog safety and life planning.

Family matters may cause disturbances with dog ownership. The leading issue is the separation of relationships. Divorce or couple separation affects not only the spouses and children, but the family dog as well. Who will get the dog? Will the family home be sold? Where will the dog live, if both parties are forced to move?

Children create family situations of their own. Parents may dearly want a dog, but children do not always agree with their parents. Scenarios such as: breed choice, animal preference and gender selection may all play roles in pet decisions. The kids may want a small dog, rather than a larger one. Parents may choose a female, whereas the kids wanted a male. The kids wanted a cat, but the parents wanted a dog. Parents and kids must form a mutual decision.

Medical problems may arise. Many children may discover allergy issues. Children who have not been pre-exposed could show signs of allergic reactions to new pups. These cases may require rehousing the pup; however most breeders will allow a pup return.

Financial issues cause several issues with dog maintenance. People are not educated regarding dog expenses: medical, housing, nutrition, training, and educational. Vet bills can be costly: reproduction control, annual inoculations and emergency necessities are difficult hardships. Housing responsibilities can be demanding; additional fees may be charged by land lords for allowing dogs. Preparing homes can add up quickly; fencing, kennels, and yard guards are not cheap materials. Measures required to provide adequate safety and security for your dog can accumulate very rapidly; dogs aren't cheap, but they are worth it.

Nutritional concerns are a valid expense. Most owners are prepared for typical nutritional requirements, but dogs coping with unusual necessities may accelerate additional costs. The price tags for specific foods are quite a bit more than owners expect. Biting off more than one can chew is an uncomfortable situation.

Educational expenses are stressful for finances. Training classes may be very costly. Behavioral problems may result in a need for additional courses or training sessions. Training is a preventative and a post solution remedy for behavioral issues.

The causes of neglect and abuse have been addressed in the above overview. These causes have led to a critical need for shelters and rescues. Society created this need, now who within our society will step forward to solve or aid in the solution for this horrific problem?

Governing, designing and operating a rescue is a very complex business. There are numerous considerations involved: expenses, regulations, staff, medical, insurances and yet so much more. Rescues or shelters are operated under the supervision of multiple control factors: state regulations, city or town ordinances, local humane societies and additional clubs or foundations. Please research this industry for more detailed information; designating the location of choice and rescue business format will guide specific outlines which must be honored.

Rescues are not for cases of neglect and abuse alone. Facilities capable of assisting owners with medical treatment programs serve as liaisons or agencies of love. Owners do not have to abandon their "best friends" thanks to the assistance programs provided by these organizations.

Providing the medical care is the first step along the care provision pathway. Rescues and/or shelters encourage a well-rounded system of treatment, recovery and reassociation. These avenues are addressed by program leads or field specialists. The medical expert team may consist of: veterinarians, social workers, physical therapists, and trainers. All members truly have the dog's best interests at heart.

Shelters of smaller size or lower budgets deserve society's respect and gratitude. These facilities make a loving difference to numerous animals in need. The shelters provide limited health care, nutritional provisions, specialized attention, and restricted training. The level or amount of care may be less due to financial situations, but the facilities work very hard to respond to the animal's needs with a respectful hand. Many of these shelters are maintained by private families

The Golden Retriever Rescue of America states its promissory oath to be one of heart felt respect, honor, love and rebirthing. Step by step, all rescues begin with a true dedication of love, respect and consideration towards the dog. Every dog must be evaluated for its individualistic needs before determining the rescue or shelter's capability to provide appropriate care.

Evaluations involve: medical examination, temperament review, and current or previous ownership when available. Rescue or shelter placement is determined based on specific dog needs verses rescue or shelter capabilities. Once the screening collaboration has been completed, the treatment process kicks into gear.

Veterinarians may be contracted to conduct thorough examinations on every dog. Medical examinations will determine the overall health of the dog. Many dogs are abandoned because the owner cannot or will not cope with a medical demand. The financial stress related to medical care plays a significant role; those incapable of providing care feel abandonment to be their only choice.

Medical examinations uncover numerous findings: accidental injuries, genetic diseases, ownership abuse, malnutrition, behavioral issues, and general illness. The dog may have sustained an injury: traffic accident, dog fight, personal fall, etc... Treating such injuries may be expensive. For example, Sandra earns a respectful wage as a clerk; however, her income could not support the care her dog required due to a car striking her dog. Dogs do not carry insurance, the owner must be responsible; unfortunately, an owner may dearly love their dog, but cannot afford such a tragedy. Veterinarians rarely allow payment arrangements; a small margin of vets will recommend credit agencies which will promote short term loans; however, these creditors may charge high interest or require superior credit scores. This scenario may call for the aid of a well-established high functioning rescue capable of providing financial assistance.

There are rare cases in which the dog may be forced to cope with a genetic disease: heart issues, hip dysplasia, retinal dysfunction . . . etc. Medical treatments such as: surgery, medications, and physical therapy may be required; these health aids are wonderful miracles that carry an awful price tag. Owners may love their pet, but be incapable of financial support. This incident may call for the aid of a senior rescue willing to provide financial assistance.

The opposite side of this issue truly strikes society's heart. Owners who abuse their pets, then abandon them should be punished. Humane societies, veterinarian agencies, and private individuals note horrific abuse cases every day. Those responsible for causing harm to an animal are subject to regional specific laws. Rescues follow legal regulations to investigate, remove, and provide care for these needy animals.

Rescues and/or shelters share common goals. These facilities set three basic goals: a promise to provide: love, attention, nutrition, and exercise. The facilities hope to promote educational training for the correction and or advancement of dog behavioral. Experts wish is to relocate these wonderful creatures into positive roles to enjoy a happy and healthy life.

Personal Reflection

"Two angels on Earth"

Dogs are like humans in that they are each unique characters beholding of their very own individuality and personality. This may draw to a legendary adage "no two snowflakes are identical". Just as every human has their very own fingerprints so do dogs have their very own pawprints. All of this philosophy adds up to one incredible truth; our son Brian Douglas Bauer and his golden Azmirelda are certainly two of the most rare, eccentric, intelligent, zany, altruistic souls to grace our amazing Earth. Hand to paw, paw to hand, heart to heart, these two incredibly unique characters make the most magnificent happy go lucky twosome ever to be paired in the dog vs human world.

Allow us to tell you a little bit about our son. Friends and family have graciously labeled Brian to be an angel on Earth. He is a very generous, thoughtful, innocent, respectful old soul. Brian embraces life with great ambition and fortitude. This young man carries a warm spirit who is accepting of everyone and everything; his objectivity and zest welcome new adventures and experiences with amazing vitality and ingenuity. Is he perfect as his parents we would say yes, but in reality it is obviously no. He definitely has a few goofy quirks, peculiar interests and outstanding ideas, but these are the traits that make this angel a human therefore creating our angel on Earth. It is his very welcoming and wonderful personality that so tenderly embraced our precious golden retriever pup, Azmarelda.

Azmirelda was born into a very large litter of golden retriever pups. She was not only one amongst her litter of eleven, but she was the one. This little miss was the one puppy to always stray away from the others. She would patiently await her turn to nurse, never pushing another sibling out of the way. She was the little darling who cuddled up to her mama's cheek snuggling right under her ear. While all the other puppies cuddled up to mama's belly and chest, she chose her own precious little spot. It was highly noted that this pup was very observant, respectful, curious, cautious and timid. It wasn't that she was a scaredy cat, no no she was a very inquisitive pooch who pondered her every move. The old saying "better safe then sorry" was Azmirelda's motto. It was adorable to monitor this litter, noting that Azmirelda joyfully played with all of her siblings but was certain to restrain from risky situations. She seemed to get her most enjoyment from watching her siblings make fools of themselves. For example, the first time the litter got to play outside one pup at a time rushed into the little pool to cool off with a splish splash lets have some fun. Azmirelda sat on the sidelines watching everyone else get wet she so wanted to play with the rest slowly creeping up to the poolside then cautiously backing up when a few drops of water hit her, she was just too scared to take the plunge "two steps forward three steps back". A few weeks later the pups go to visit the lake, all the other puppies had been acclimated to the water, but not Azmirelda, she was petrified shaking like a leaf. This little beauty tinkled with every step she took towards the water, suddenly she bolted with fear rushing all the way back to the vehicle. It had become obvious that this precious little pup needed human intervention. Who better to comfort her soul and teach her the true value of new experiences than the most tender hearted happy go lucky super smart human on this Earth, yes she needed the best of the best and that was Brian.

Their adventure begins; Brian and Azmirelda shared an amazing uniqueness and charm all their own. Learning and growing together would definitely be a labor of love. Brian quickly realized that he could not rush or push Azmarelda into anything; her training would definitely be a step by step process requiring intense consideration and dedication. Don't get us wrong; she learned quickly and advanced better than the majority of our golden retriever pups. The key to her success definitely rested within Brian's heart. He had to handle Azmirelda with the utmost respect and biggest heart if he wanted her to achieve her training goals. Praise was his best tool; she lives for his admiration and approval. Brian could never raise his voice or use too sharp of a tone as it would only result in his soft hearted golden slipping away with the walk of shame, hurt and abandon. Once her heart had been broken it could take weeks to reclaim her trust. We truly believe our son was the perfect teacher for this golden student; as his own teachers at school could've compared his personality to Azmirelda's. Brian lived life with a very tender heart that could easily be wounded if not handled with gentle and respectful guidance. Brian has matured with tremendous integrity and character as he is a very intelligent young man accomplishing honor society status along his pathway to criminal justice. We truly believe that he trained her in the same manner his own heart and soul demanded. Therefore two gentle yet brave hearts beat as one.

Obedience 1-2 had been achieved; this golden retriever pup was really proving herself. Brian was a very proud teacher. The twosome were ready to undergo Obedience 3, trick training and advanced skills. Training at this level is definitely more challenging, requiring: intelligence, patience, repetition, consistency, and trust. They began with a few easier going tricks: paw, down, settle, and give. These tasks were quickly and easily conquered leading them into the next set of tricks and skills: focus fetch, roll over, sit pretty, figure eight, and road safety. Being that these tasks involved a significant amount of trust we were shocked that she faced them with confidence, clarity, and charisma. It was obvious that Azmirelda was brilliant, definitely beholding skills above and beyond the typical pet level. We were well aware Brian must remain her number one trainer, but it was also time to welcome an assistant who was highly skilled in additional arenas which would draw out this golden's incredible capabilities.

Bruce and Brian paired to introduce the arena of hunting to Ms Azmirelda. She was absolutely intrigued with her new training opportunity. Brian prompted Bruce to approach every training session with a big heart, soft voice, and gentle smile as he knew his dog, his best friend, required a loving heart to learn. She enjoyed playing with the pheasant wings, advanced fetch was more then a game, it grew into an amazing skill. They were a family working together and playing together making hunting life a great success.

Recognizing Azmirelda's outstanding skills in hunting lead to opening the door to yet another arena, behavioral servicing. Altering many of the tasks a hunting dog performs into skills a service dog performs was actually an easy transformation. Azmirelda's soul had a beautiful love for children. Bruce and Brian enjoyed teaching her many behavioral skills: block, cover, corral, massage, alert, and many more; all of which would grant tremendous assistance to autistic children in the future. Never breaking the golden rule. That by teaching Azmirelda with a big heart, soft voice and gentle smile a true miracle, that being miracle dog would truly blossom. Azmirelda beholding many precious traits was definitely destined to pass her outstanding genetics and incredible gifts to the next generation. Motherhood has been her truest blessing, a treasure she shares with many puppy to puppy. Is Azmirelda perfect as her family we would say yes, but obviously no, however, she is our golden angel on earth.

Acknowledgements

We would like to acknowledge our fellow golden retriever enthusiasts. Loving a golden is truly a blessing. Our heartfelt respect and gratitude is expressed to all those who breed, raise, employ, train, handle, own and rescue goldens. Thank you all for sharing life with these magnificent creatures.

Preparing a book involves a great deal of work. We would like to thank the medical experts who granted us numerous interviews. The collection of facts, records, and materials assured the quality we demanded. The material within this book has been respectfully assessed, organized, and edited by two very knowledgeable and resourceful assistants: Julia Shaw and Rebecca Hallin. The many heart to heart discussions shared with breeders, trainers and handlers provided an incredible wealth of information; our book could not have reached its intellectual and emotional peeks without their influence. Club members and private owners added a perfect touch of family class. All in all, the human contact research conducted for this book proves, that goldens truly are man's best friend and Man is truly a golden's best friend!

Educational appreciation is respectfully expressed to our numerous resources portrayed throughout this book. We urge our readers to conduct their own research to confirm the quality of our investigation. Golden retriever facts are updated on a rapid basis; therefore, advancements are reported to the public at superior rates. Learning with and about goldens has been an honor.

The spectacular pictures shared throughout this book are thanks to our amazing daughter Breanna Bauer. Her remarkable skills and considerate heart captured the gorgeous appearance and loving hearts of our family of goldens. Please allow us to share our original family of goldens: Sir Alexander Kaden Bauer the Great, Abagale Karicia Ruby and Anastacia Kimberli Rose. We will then joyfully share the lives of our breathtaking goldens as they appear along our family lifeline.

Sir Alexander Kaden Bauer the Great thoroughly enjoyed posing for Breanna's shots; catching him off guard presented the best pictures. Our dames: Abagale Karicia Ruby and Anastacia Kimberli Rose felt like princesses as they showed off for the camera. Breanna had her work cut out for her as the human and dog families merged for group shots. We all enjoyed "strutting our stuff". Breanna's skill and heart truly honor the saying, "a picture is worth a thousand words".

Our talented daughter definitely poured her heart and soul into capturing many precious moments with all of our golden family members. She focused on every stage of their lives never skipping a heartbeat in their lives. She is definitely the reason every one of our goldens are little hams. The most fun comes from the goldens photo bombing each other.

Researching, writing and reading this book have been the enjoyable steps along the publishing process. The editing lay out, and revisions are the tedious work. Special thanks to a dear friend, Rebecca Hallin for her incredible assistance, patience and consideration throughout the production of "Precious Pet of Gold". A huge thank you is respectfully granted to my niece/goddaughter Julia Shaw for her impeccable spirit, intelligence, consideration as she assisted throughout every step of our production pathway. It is thanks to them that this material is presented in an intelligent and interesting manner for your educational enjoyment.

Every book calls for a unique touch of class; achieving this creative obstacle was actually quite intriguing. Many avenues were approached, but set aside. We truly wanted to embrace a stimulant which we thought would reach out and grab our reading audience. Realizing it was time to think out of the box the search was on for unreproachable eccentricities. "A picture may say a thousand words", yet though pictures are precious they alone did not fulfill our mission. Explosive rare talent was the edge we needed to put this book over the top. Introducing our readers' captor, artist Jeffrey Lyn Shaw II. Please truly behold, enjoy, and grasp the many pleasures within each of the caricatures within this book.

It has been a great honor to produce this book. Owning golden retrievers is a lifelong gift. Learning with them has been an educational process we will appreciate throughout our lives. Sharing our knowledge with our readers has been a tremendous privilege. We dearly thank our family, friends, experts, and goldens for granting us this opportunity. Our hope is that this book will mean as much to our readers as it has to us.

Personal Reflection

"Everyone is precious"

Bauer family Goldens is truly blessed to share our lives with our: Golden Retrievers, recipient families, dedicated trainers, and fellow breeders. We believe that Golden Retrievers behold the amazing ability to enhance numerous arenas within the overall spectrum of life. We would like to share with you a brief yet very meaningful glance into the lives of two precious Bauer family Golden members: Arorah and Amilia.

Arorah and Amilia are half sisters, sharing a wonderful genetic foundation from their father, Kuhn Dachelet. Arorah Elizabeth Bauer born June 11, 2017, and Amilia Mae Bauer born April 17, 2018 were purchased for their impeccable breed lines, temperaments, and physical attributes. Please allow us to touch upon each of their lives.

Arorah, selected by our beautiful daughter Maranda is a beautiful deep red golden who enjoys her dual careers: motherhood and search and rescue. She has a great love of the outdoors expressing tremendous energy as she proves her search and rescue skills along numerous trails, crime scenes, and recreational hikes. The most amazing accomplishment Arorah has achieved is her ability to locate a missing child from Madison WI. Arorah was very familiar with a four year old Down syndrome boy as she had accompanied the family on many hikes as a respite assistant. The family contacted us with awful news that their little boy had been missing for several hours. We had volunteered to bring Arorah to their home in hopes she could track his location. Authorities led her to his room to gather his scent and set her in motion. A very heart wrenching clock ticked away as she went to work yard to yard, house to house, searching for the little boy. It seemed like eternity however in reality only a few hours had passed when Arorah found the little boy hiding in a neighbor's abandoned dog house. The little boy was sound asleep and very safe. She alerted authority proving her skills as a superior search and rescue dog. She proved her love of children by snuggling and cuddling the little boy so he wasn't afraid of the crowd that awaited him. Her love of human children extends to a deep love of her own puppies. She truly enjoys motherhood as she teaches her pups to appreciate every part of nature; sharing life with her has been such an honor.

Amilia has been dubbed the "teddy bear" of Golden Retrievers. She dearly loves children! This beautiful Golden girl has such a huge heart that she attaches her spirit to every child within her grasp. Bauer family goldens have been blessed by Amilia's mothering skills, having birthed many gorgeous litters that have touched the lives of many recipients. Her deep love of our granddaughters Stormy and Skylar led to an early retirement of her breeding arena, but it opened the door to her sharing her life and love with them in their home as their full-time best friend and surrogate mom.

Bauer family goldens truly respects and loves every golden family member. It has been and shall continue to be a privilege to share our lives with each and every one of our golden retrievers. We are a family of humans and golden retrievers, each of us are unique individuals beholding exclusive qualities and characteristics that blend, enhance, encourage, and touch one another's lives thus sharing an incredible pathway through life. Thank you for joining us along our adventure.